# You Made It, Now What?

## A College Student's Guide to Success

Brian J. Gorman, Ed.D.

Jennifer L. Roth-Burnette, Ph.D.

**Kendall Hunt** publishing company

Cover image © Shutterstock, Inc.

**Kendall Hunt**
publishing company

www.kendallhunt.com
*Send all inquiries to*
4050 Westmark Drive
Dubuque, IA 52004-1840

Copyright © 2021 by Kendall Hunt Publishing Company

ISBN 978-1-7924-9020-0

Published in the United States of America

# TABLE OF CONTENTS

**Chapter 5:     Building your Success Toolkit   133**

## Chapter 1

# Getting Settled and Starting Strong

| Choices of Successful Students | Choices of Struggling Students |
|---|---|
| 1. Assume responsibility for their college success. | 1. Place responsibility for their college success on others, especially their professors. |
| 2. Take steps to be prepared for classes *before* they begin by identifying locations and acquiring materials. | 2. Wait until after classes have started to start identifying locations and acquiring materials, missing important pieces at the beginning. |
| 3. Work to cultivate passion and perseverance toward specific goals to succeed in college. | 3. Meander through the college experience without identifying or establishing goals from the outset. |
| 4. Take on a "creator" mindset and avoid being a victim. | 4. Maintain a "victim" mindset by blaming others, or avoiding their challenges entirely. |
| 5. Are intentional about maintaining pre-college relationships that are beneficial to their success, while letting go of those that are not. | 5. Allow unhealthy or overbearing pre-college relationships to continue to a point they become a barrier to achieving their goals. |
| 6. Read all syllabi thoroughly to understand what is expected in each class and how they will be assessed. | 6. Fail to read their syllabi and as a result are confused about what they need to learn or accomplish in each class. |
| 7. Write important deadlines, tests, and class requirements in their calendars or planners and consult their calendars or planners daily. | 7. Don't use a calendar, planner or other system to stay organized, and end up missing important deadlines, tests, and other class requirements. |
| 8. Access and learn at least the basics of their college or university's Student Code of Conduct. | 8. Ignore their college or university's Student Code of Conduct and eventually violate it. |
| 9. Learn common forms of inside or outside of the classroom incivility, and actively avoid them. | 9. Continue common practices of college incivility, disrupting the experience of others. |

## Welcome!

Welcome to the next great adventure of your life! You have worked hard all of your academic life and have made it to college, now what? Whether you are coming to college straight from high school, took some time off from schooling to explore other opportunities, or are enrolling in a new college or university, a new and exciting journey full of opportunities is about to begin!

If you have ever been an athlete, you may have been told by a coach to "set the tone" for the game. I know that when I was a high school football coach, I used to tell my offensive lineman and linebackers to "set the tone." Get off the ball and hit them hard, set the tone by letting them know you are here to be physical. I would tell linebackers to bring their pads and set the tone for the ball carriers, letting them know it would be a long, arduous night for them. The same goes for students entering college. Students need to set the tone for themselves and get in to a routine of habits, behaviors, and thought processes that are going to lead to college success, and they should do so right away. Your first semester in college is going to be full of new opportunities academically and socially which provides a lot of excitement, but also distractions. Research indicates that the first college semester is often students' most challenging, not because they are taking their most difficult classes, but because they are learning much about themselves and their new environment. This book will help you start off on a pathway toward college success, and graduation."

– Dr. Brian Gorman

As you enter college you should expect to take the most difficult classes you have ever taken. Every year we have students ask why they have to take public speaking, algebra, or biology when they have already taken it in high school. Students sometimes don't realize that they may take many of the "same" subjects as they did in high school. This is good for familiarity with the subject, but students need to understand that the college level of these subjects will be more advanced. The good news is that you wouldn't have been accepted to your college or university if they didn't think you could be successful. In fact, you may have beat out thousands of other applicants for your spot. The question is, will you make the choices that lead to college success? If you follow the recommendations of this book, you will.

It is time to make a choice: what kind of college student will you be? Will you be a high achiever and choose to go to class every day, choose to turn in all of your assignments, choose to do assigned readings and look at lecture notes even if you don't have an assignment due? Many students haven't thought about this before arriving to college, assuming they will do what they did in previous schooling and be fine. That very well may be the case, but now is the time to take a hard look at your previous study habits and decide if they will be enough to achieve your long-term college and career goals.

### Focus Questions:

1. What is college success, and how can this book help me achieve it?
2. What are some important concepts that will help me set the tone for my college success?
3. What habits and thought processes should you bring to college, and which do you leave behind?

## What is College Success?

Throughout this book you will often hear the term "college success." When we use this term, we are referring to *you* achieving *your* goals which may include earning a high grade point average (GPA), never having to drop or withdraw from a class, completing your Associate's degree at a community college and transferring to a 4-year college or university, returning to complete a college degree, or graduating in four years. No matter your definition of college success, this book will be helpful in achieving it.

## How to Use this Book

In this book, we offer support and guidance to help you find success and satisfaction in your college experience. We'll walk you through the process of planning effectively, avoiding pitfalls, and taking good care of yourself. If and when you do stumble, we'll share strategies for picking yourself back up and moving forward.

This book is not just for reading, but for *doing*. You'll get out of it what you put into it. We encourage you to thoughtfully consider and respond to the discovery and focus questions throughout each chapter. These are designed to help you identify your own thought processes and experiences in ways that will make the information we present more valuable and applicable to you.

We also strongly recommend you complete the activities within, and at the end of each chapter. These are opportunities for you to practice and hone the skills you will need to be a successful college student. Each end-of-chapter activity is designed to be applicable and adaptable to you – your schedule, your classes, your talents, your preferences, your life. As you read through each chapter, look for this symbol to see which topics have related end-of-chapter activities:

© Iyovajan/Shutterstock.com

If you are using this book in preparation for attending college, and aren't actually experiencing a college term while reading it, all of the activities are useful practice. For some activities you may need to go to your college or university's website to find specific information, or participate in the activity as just practice for when you arrive to college. Practice makes perfect!

If you are using this book during your college experience, the chapter order flows along with your academic term. Chapters 1 and 2 present strategies for starting your college experience successfully, with additional resources and midterm preparation in Chapter 3. Chapter 4 provides strategies for getting involved with student life outside of the classroom. Chapters 5 and 6 go deeper into academic and personal development, and Chapter 7 focuses on finishing your academic term strong. If you are working through this book over a 15-week term, we suggest working through the chapters in 2-week intervals, spreading each chapter over a couple of weeks. If you are enrolled in a 10-week term, we suggest working through a chapter every week, and building in extra time (1.5–2 weeks each) for the denser materials in Chapters 5 and 6.

If you need help right away with specific topics like Note-Taking or Mindful Practices we encourage you to use the table of contents in the front of the book, or the index in the back to jump ahead to those topics as you need them!

Succeeding in college has everything to do with being focused and determined, cultivating a positive mindset, and developing good habits from the outset. The steps presented in this book, taken seriously, will set you on the road to a successful academic term.

© atk work/Shutterstock.com

## Getting Ready for Your First Week of Classes

There's a lot to do, to get ready for classes! In order to be prepared and self-assured, complete the following steps during the week or so before classes begin:

1. **Check your class schedule.** This may sound obvious, but students often sign up for classes months before an academic term begins and may not check their schedule until the first day of classes. Sometimes they find out that their schedule isn't what they remember. College classes can sometimes be cancelled, and while students enrolled in those classes are usually notified by email, sometimes they aren't checking their university email regularly yet. Make sure your class schedule is what you expect, and check it before the first day of classes.

2. **Locate your classes.** If your classes are meeting on campus, get a campus map and start identifying the buildings and locations. Even better, take a walk and find them physically so you can feel confident navigating to your first day of classes. If your classes are back-to-back and your campus is large, you may have to hurry to get to your next class on time. Don't be late to your first class because you got lost trying to find it! If your classes are online, go ahead and get familiar with the online system you will use to access them.

3. **Download and print the syllabus for each class.** At most colleges, syllabi will be available online before your classes start, and being familiar with your syllabus will help you know ahead of time the name of the faculty, their office location, how to contact them, what textbooks and materials are needed, and the location of your class, as well as what the class requirements are, and how your learning will be assessed. Tips for navigating your college syllabi are found later in this chapter.

4. **Purchase or rent required textbooks and other materials for each class.** These can typically be found at your college bookstore, where they will be identified by class and instructor. Many college bookstores have online textbook purchase options as well! In addition, many college texts are available new, used, and online. Check your syllabus to see whether your instructor has chosen a particular medium for your text (for instance, online or printed copy). If you have the choice, choose the medium that is most likely to work best for you.

---

*If you decide to purchase from an online retail bookstore, be aware that different editions might have the same author and title. Be sure that you purchase a book with the ISBN that matches the one for your required text. You can run into problems if, for example, you are assigned the 8th edition of a book and you purchase the 3rd edition.*

---

5. **Get set for taking notes.** In college, you'll need to take notes in class as well as on your assigned readings, videos and other materials. Whether you plan to take notes on paper or on a laptop or tablet, go to class prepared to take notes beginning on the first day. If you will be using paper, think about whether you will be best served by a ream of loose-leaf notebook paper that you can organize into folders or notebooks, or by keeping a composition notebook for each class you take. Composition notebooks are generally inexpensive and are a great way to keep your notes on each class together. Consider what you prefer to write with – do you prefer a mechanical pencil, a standard lead pencil, a gel pen or a ball point pen? Select the writing implement that you will most enjoy and that works best for you.

6. **Decide how you will stay organized.** Choose the type of calendar and/or planner you will use to keep yourself organized this academic term. You might enjoy perusing your local office supply or campus bookstore for a variety of planners you could choose from. *For more information on time management strategies and materials, see the segment below on Time Management.*

7. **Get in the habit of checking your campus email daily.** Your college or university assigned email is the primary way university faculty and staff will communicate with you. All are important messages from your college or university and may include topics like the cancelling of a class, a time-sensitive message from a professor, or information on your financial aid or bill. Not checking your campus email daily can lead to it piling up quickly, and missing important messages along the way.

"My first piece of advice is to really use syllabus week to get organized. If you use a planner to insert all class times and important due dates at the beginning, you will be able to more easily update your planner each week. You should also use this time to organize school supplies in a way that works for you. Another tip I have is to be sure to know where all your classes are. Some class buildings may be super familiar, but if not be sure to scope out the classroom beforehand; that way you do not run late the first day. Additionally, during the first week of classes be sure to fully unpack your living situation. I know a lot of time people move in right before the semester starts, so it is important get your home for the year in order before you really start digging into content for your classes. This will help reduce stress as classes begin overall."

— Mae F., freshman, Management

## Grit, and Why it Matters

Dr. Angela Duckworth, in *Grit: The Power of Passion and Perseverance*, describes her many years of research into what makes people, including students, successful. She has determined that talent, test scores and innate ability are *not* the best predictors of success. Rather, the students who are most likely to achieve their academic goals are those with a combination of **passion** (commitment and devotion to their goals) and **perseverance** (continuing to work toward their goals even with faced with difficulties) that Duckworth describes as *grit*.

© iQoncept/Shutterstock.com

Dr. Duckworth and others who study the relationship between talent and achievement find, over and over, that hard work matters considerably more than talent or innate ability when it comes to predicting success. Duckworth points out that people who work hard at developing their skills are also *practicing* those skills repeatedly in the process of learning them, so they are more secure in their abilities, and they are more productive in the long run.

Will Smith, Grammy Award-winning musician and Oscar-nominated actor, shares this perspective on talent, effort, skill and achievement (Will Smith Interview: Will Power, p. 95):

*"I consider myself to be of basically average talent, right? What I have that other people do not have is a sick, obsessive, raw animal drive. There is no pain worse than not achieving a dream when it is your fault.... If you do not get what you desire because you are lazy, there is no pain worse than that."*

Will Smith goes on to say,

*"The key to life is on a treadmill. When I say I am going to run three miles, I run five. With that mentality, it is actually difficult to lose."*

---

**DISCOVERY**

1. What skills have I developed through hard work in my life so far?

   _____

   _____

   _____

2. What skills do I need to work hard to improve on in order to succeed in college?

   _____

   _____

   _____

---

## How Gritty Are You?

Complete the following questionnaire to find your current "grit" score. Read each sentence and then circle the number that describes you. Don't overthink these questions, just consider how you think you compare to "most people."

| | Not at all like me | Not much like me | Somewhat like me | Mostly like me | Very much like me |
|---|---|---|---|---|---|
| 1. I am sometimes distracted from my current projects when new projects come along | 5 | 4 | 3 | 2 | 1 |
| 2. I am not easily discouraged by setbacks. | 1 | 2 | 3 | 4 | 5 |
| 3. After setting one goal, I often choose to pursue a different one. | 5 | 4 | 3 | 2 | 1 |
| 4. I am someone who works hard. | 1 | 2 | 3 | 4 | 5 |
| 5. If a project takes more than a few months to complete, I am likely to lose focus. | 5 | 4 | 3 | 2 | 1 |

*(Continued...)*

| | Not at all like me | Not much like me | Somewhat like me | Mostly like me | Very much like me |
|---|---|---|---|---|---|
| 6. When I begin something, I am determined to finish it. | 1 | 2 | 3 | 4 | 5 |
| 7. My interests seem to change every year. | 5 | 4 | 3 | 2 | 1 |
| 8. I don't give up. I keep working toward my goals. | 1 | 2 | 3 | 4 | 5 |
| 9. Sometimes I am extremely focused on one project for a short while, and later lose interest. | 5 | 4 | 3 | 2 | 1 |
| 10. I have managed to overcome difficulties to accomplish something challenging. | 1 | 2 | 3 | 4 | 5 |

Adapted from Angela Duckworth, *Grit: The Power of Passion and Perseverance* (2016).

Calculate your grit score by adding up all the points for the boxes you checked, then divide the total by 10. The maximum score for this scale is 5, "extremely gritty" and the lowest possible score is 1, "not at all gritty."

My grit score _____

*You may also take the Grit Scale questionnaire online at Angela Duckworth's website, https://angeladuckworth.com/grit-scale/*

Use the following chart to see how your scores compare to a large sample of American adults. Based on the chart below, for instance, if you scored a 3.9 then you are grittier than 60% of the adults sampled by Dr. Duckworth.

| Percentile | Grit score | Percentile | Grit score |
|---|---|---|---|
| 10% | 2.5 | 70% | 4.1 |
| 20% | 3.0 | 80% | 4.3 |
| 30% | 3.3 | 90% | 4.5 |
| 40% | 3.5 | 95% | 4.7 |
| 50% | 3.8 | 99% | 4.9 |
| 60% | 3.9 | | |

Your grit score is a reflection of how you see yourself *right now*, and will likely change over time. If you scored "gritty" (3.9 or higher) then you have already developed some of the passion and perseverance that will help you be a successful college student. If your grit score was lower, don't worry! Grit grows with age and experience, and you can work to develop it. College is an excellent place and time to be building your academic and personal skills and your grit.

## Grit and Goals

In order to have grit, you have to start with goals. The grittiest individuals in Duckworth's research are those who had defined their goals clearly, and whose most important (or top-level) goals did not change over a long period of time. Furthermore, those individuals' less important (low-level and mid-level) goals were typically connected to their top-level goals. For instance, a person whose most important goal was to graduate with a specific major in four years might have mid-level goals to pass every class each term to stay on track for their degree, and low-level goals to commit to weekly study. If that person did not pass one particular class, they might shift their plans to retake the class in a summer term in order to stay on track for their main goal of completing the college degree in a specified amount of time.

> "My first piece of advice is to start the semester by setting a list of goals. This can include things such as grades you want to achieve, clubs and organizations you want to join, contributions you want to make to your clubs and organizations, social goals, and more. It is good to start the semester with a big picture in mind of how you want things to go. Another piece of advice is to get organized by getting either a planner or calendar and inputting all your assignments and exam dates as you get them during syllabus week. This will allow you to plan accordingly for the upcoming semester. You also want to make sure you have all the books and supplies needed for your classes. It is best to get everything organized the first week or two before everything gets hectic. It is easy to fall behind during the first few weeks because students may think they can put off the first bit of work and studying they have to do. It is important to keep up with your work and studying as you go to ensure you are not having to cram before a test or assignment is due."
>
> — Payton M., senior, Psychology

## DISCOVERY

1. What is an example of a goal I worked hard for and achieved in the past? How long did I work on that goal? What was the outcome?

   _____

   _____

   _____

2. What is my top goal right now, as a college student?

   _____

   _____

   _____

3. How long do I expect it to take for me to reach my goal?

   _____

   _____

   _____

4. What are the mid- and low-level goals that will help me achieve my top goal?

   _____

   _____

   _____

5. What strengths do I possess that will help me stay focused on my top goal and my lower or mid-level goals?

   _____

   _____

   _____

# College vs. High School

If you are entering college for the first time after high school, you will probably notice that college offers you greater independence, but also requires greater responsibility. If you are transferring from a two-year college or returning to your studies after a hiatus, you probably have some idea of what to expect, though the four-year college experience may be new to you. Read through the following chart and consider which of these differences you have already experienced:

| High School | College |
|---|---|
| **YOUR SCHEDULE** | |
| You spent 6–7 hours each day – 30 hours per week – in class, going directly from one class to the next. | You spend 12–16 hours per week in class, usually with breaks in between. Your classes might be at any time of day or evening. |

| High School | College |
|---|---|
| Your guidance counselor arranged your class schedule for you. | You arrange your own class schedule in consultation with an academic advisor. Your schedule may look lighter than it actually is. |
| Your school year was 36 weeks long, with a long winter holiday break, a short spring break, and a long summer break. | Your academic year is divided into two 15-week semesters, or three 10-week trimesters, with an exam week at the end of each. You may also be able to take classes during a shorter summer term, or during spring or winter interim terms. |
| **YOUR CLASSES AND LEARNING** | |
| Your classes were probably no larger than 35 students and were taught by teachers. | College class sizes may range from 15 to 100s of students. Classes are taught by instructors and professors, who will be referred to as "Doctor" if they have earned a doctoral degree in their chosen field. Classes may also be taught by graduate assistants. |
| Your teachers presented materials to help you understand the textbook, often writing information on the board or projecting a power point for you to copy into your notes. | Professors may lecture nonstop, give illustrations, offer background information, or discuss research about the topics you are studying. You will be expected to take notes on a variety of materials and to be up to date on all assigned readings. |
| Your time was structured by others: administrators, teachers, coaches, parents and family. Teachers monitor class attendance. | You manage your own time. It is up to you to go to class, complete assigned readings, take notes, and study. Professors may or may not formally take roll, but your attendance will still matter in terms of your ability to participate and learn the material. |
| You were told what you needed to learn from assigned readings and you may have received reminders of assignments and due dates. Teachers check your completed work. | Professors expect you to use your syllabus, which spells out what is expected of you, when it is due and how it will be graded. It is your responsibility to read and understand the material. Lectures and assignments are based on the assumption that you have done so. |
| Teachers may have approached you if they believed you needed assistance. | Professors will typically be open and helpful, but will expect you to initiate contact when you need assistance (by attending their office hours, or email, for instance). They will also expect you to use campus resources like the Academic Success Center, Writing Center, and Libraries. |
| You may have had short reading assignments to discuss in class, or homework you needed to complete before class. | You will have substantial reading assignments which may or may not be discussed in class. You will need to study on average 2–3 hours outside of class for each hour you spend in class, to keep up with the coursework. |

(Continued...)

| High School | College |
|---|---|
| Testing was frequent and covered small amounts of material. You may have had review sessions in which teachers pointed out important concepts. | Testing is infrequent (possibly only 2 or 3 exams or tests each semester). You are expected to organize your own material to prepare for tests. Professors may or may not offer review sessions, and if they do, they expect you to come prepared with questions. Makeup tests are rarely an option. You need to be prepared and on time to your tests and exams. |
| You were probably able to graduate as long as you passed all required courses with a D or higher. | You may graduate only if your average in classes meets the departmental standard, which is usually a 2.0 or a C. |
| **MANAGING YOURSELF** | |
| You needed permission to participate in extracurricular activities. | You decide whether to participate in co-curricular activities. |
| Your living expenses were likely paid for, and your textbooks were probably provided at little or no expense. You needed money for special activities, gas, and trips. | If you live on campus you will need to pay for housing and dining in advance of each semester. You may also need to budget significant funds for textbooks, and you will need your own computer or will need to be sure you can access a computer lab regularly for study. |
| Parents and teachers likely reminded you of your responsibilities and guided you in setting priorities. You may have been corrected if your behavior was out of line. | You are responsible for what you do and don't do, and for the consequences of those decisions. In addition to study, you will need to manage your own budget, do your own laundry and learn to live in an environment without a lot of external structure. You will be faced with moral and ethical decisions you have not had to face previously. *You* must balance your responsibilities and set priorities. |

# Tips for Making a Successful Transition to College

- Take control of your own education. Think of yourself as a scholar.
- Get to know your professors. They are one of your greatest resources.
- Be assertive. Plug into support systems and develop your network. Ask for help when you need it, and ask when you *first* need it (don't wait as things continue to get worse).
- Get to know academic support resources like your college's academic success center or tutoring center, writing center, libraries, and others.
- Take control of your time. Plan to satisfy your academic obligations and then make room for everything else.
- Make thoughtful decisions. Don't add or drop classes impulsively. Think it through and check in with your advisor.
- Think beyond the moment. Set goals for your semester, year, and college career.

### DISCOVERY

1.  Which 2 to 3 elements of the college transition do I already have well in hand?

    _____

    _____

    _____

2.  Which 2 to 3 elements of the college transition do I particularly need to be working on?

    _____

    _____

    _____

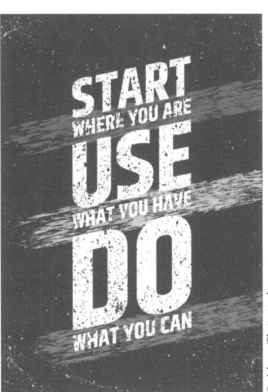

© nickmoz/Shutterstock.com

"College has taught me a lot about being self-sufficient and independent. My biggest adjustment was being so far away from family and friends, and really trying to navigate my way through a completely different culture and environment. College kind of taught me to start over in many ways. I needed to throw out a lot of the self-taught behaviors I had developed for studying. I found that I had a lot of resources at my college and it would be silly not to utilize them. I spent a lot of time talking to students older than myself and really absorbed their stories and suggestions like a sponge."

— Jordan S., senior, Public Health

# Assuming Responsibility and Creating Opportunity

An important concept to understand that may be different in college than was in high school is the responsibility for your overall success, including how much you learn. Prior to college, much of your success was the responsibility of your parents or family, as well as teachers, administrators, and school districts. In college, while there are measurements in place to hold professors and colleges and universities accountable, YOU are responsible for your success and must take the steps yourself to achieve your goals. As was the case in your promotion from elementary to middle to high school, when you graduated from high school and were admitted to college you earned a promotion. You may also have been promoted in a job as well and can relate to the increases of responsibility that came with it. No matter the environment, with promotion comes increased responsibility. You are expected to assume this increased responsibility for yourself in college, and be able to take the next step toward achieving your goals. You will need to be able to problem solve, think critically, grow emotionally and socially, learn independently, and take the steps necessary to do so even when it is inconvenient or uncomfortable. You have a choice: actively take steps to earn your success, or passively float through college and allow your potential success to fade away.

Increased personal responsibility does not mean you are on your own, however, and you should plan on being interdependent by utilizing the resources your college or university provides for you. This book will take a deep dive in to a variety of college and university resources, and how you should utilize them for your success. Becoming interdependent means learning to access the resources available to you and the people who will advocate for you. Advocates at your college or university include your faculty or professors, academic advisors and coaches, counselors, and all sorts of professional staff with special expertise in concepts such as health and wellness, leadership, diversity and equity, and financial literacy.

# Avoiding a Victim Mindset

Most students who arrive to college already understand their responsibility for success and use of resources to support it. There are others, however, that often take on a Victim mindset. This concept will be covered by a variety of examples throughout the book, emphasizing how you can be proactive and take steps for improving your situation and avoiding setbacks. In an effort to help you gain an early understanding of the concept, below are some common examples of students using the Victim mindset:

- "My professor didn't answer my email so I didn't know how to complete the assignment."
- "My alarm didn't go off so I missed class."
- "My 8 a.m. class is too early."
- "My professor is a bad teacher."
- "My residence hall is too noisy for me to get any real studying done."

You may have noticed that in the above examples the student is passing blame on to someone or something else and deflecting responsibility from the student. Blame is placed on the professor, an alarm clock, the time of day a class is scheduled for, the number of hours in a day or a busy schedule, and a residence hall. The examples below are a different kind of Victim mindset in which the student identifies himself as the culprit, but insinuates there is nothing that he can do to change his circumstances.

- "I'm not good at math."
- "I couldn't find a place to park so I was late."
- "I am not interested in the lecture and can't keep attention in class."
- "I'm a procrastinator."
- "I don't have enough time to study for all of my classes."

For both sets of Victim mindset examples the student should change his focus to what actions he can take to remediate the problem. College and life skill expert Skip Downing (2017) refers to this as the Creator mindset. While the student may not be able to improve the professor's teaching ability or email response habits, or increase the number of parking spots available, the student can definitely make the choice to take action for each situation and improve her circumstances. **In the spaces below, change each of the victim statements in to Creator responses, or responses that show more active responsibility that can help solve the problem. The first three are done for you:**

| Victim Response | Creator Response |
|---|---|
| "My professor didn't answer my email so I didn't know how to complete the assignment." | "When my professor didn't respond to my email, I ask a classmate for help. Next time I will be prepared to ask questions in class." |
| "My alarm didn't go off so I missed class." | "I will get in to the habit of making sure my alarm is set before I go to bed. If necessary, I will set 2 alarms." |
| "My 8 a.m. class is too early." | "I will make sure I get to bed early enough to be able to get up for my early class, and make sure to grab a coffee on the way!" |
| "My professor is a bad teacher." | |
| "My residence hall is too noisy for me to get any real studying done." | |
| "I'm not good at math." | |
| "I couldn't find a place to park so I was late." | |
| "I am not interested in the lecture and can't keep attention in class." | |

*(Continued...)*

| Victim Response | Creator Response |
| --- | --- |
| "I'm a procrastinator." | |
| "I don't have enough time to study for all of my classes." | |

Most of us have both Victim and Creator tendencies that shape how we respond to certain situations. What is important is identifying when you are in the Victim mindset, and work to change your responses to that of a Creator. Creators drive their own success, while Victims are at the mercy of their environments.

## You Choose What to Bring with You

As you were deciding what to bring with you to college, you may have chosen a favorite item or two, plus the necessities such as bed linens, towels, clothing, and technology. You may have brought much more! Some people arrive at college with a moving truck while others come with a suitcase. It's a matter of personal choice. Some people don't move away to college at all, but continue living at home and commute to campus, or study online.

Regardless of your living situation, the choice to start college is also about moving psychologically and emotionally. This is your opportunity to decide what you will bring with you in terms of relationships, habits, and ways of thinking. If you developed good study skills in the past, bring those with you! If you had a supportive community and people who encouraged you to better yourself, bring those relationships with you by staying in touch with those people. If you were in the habit of thinking positively and working hard, definitely bring those with you.

On the other hand, if you were not a very serious student in the past, or if you thought you were not capable of success, that is a self-image you can choose to leave behind. Starting college offers you a clean slate! If some of your friends or family members tended to bring you down or caused you to doubt your abilities, you might choose, thoughtfully, to limit contact with those people. If you were in a habit of thinking negatively about yourself and lacked motivation, you can choose to leave those thoughts behind. If you had not yet learned study skills, you can start learning those now!

College is an opportunity for a fresh start. You choose what to bring with you! Choose to bring the personal qualities, habits, relationships and thought patterns that help you be a better person and a better student.

**DISCOVERY**

1. What personal qualities, habits, relationships and/or thought patterns do I want to bring with me to college?

   _____

   _____

   _____

2. What personal qualities, habits, relationships and/or thought patterns do I want to leave behind?

   _____

   _____

   _____

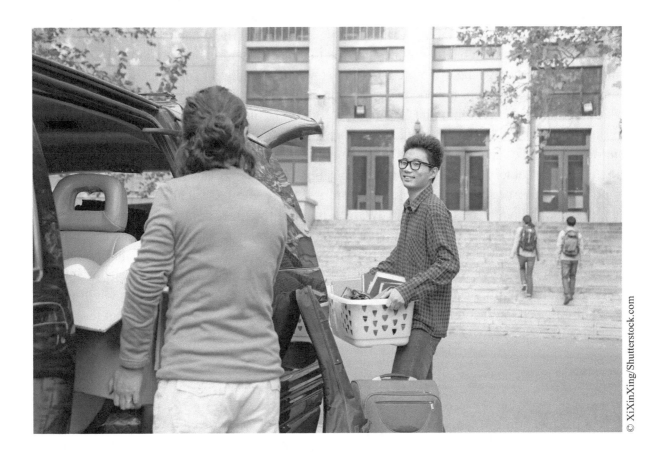

© XiXinXing/Shutterstock.com

## Managing Family and Old Friends

Coming to college for the first time is a big change in your life with many new and unfamiliar people and experiences. Staying in touch with family and friends from before you came to college provides comfort and familiarity that is helpful while you navigate the challenges and stressors of your new college or university environment. Parents, siblings, or friends who have attended college themselves may be able to serve as guides or cheerleaders for you. You should plan to remain connected to family and old friends whether you have enrolled in the college or university in or near your hometown, or branched out to a college or university thousands of miles from home. You should also consider the nature of those relationships, how often you communicate with or visit them, and if and to what extent they support your ability to achieve your goals.

As you will discover in this book, finding success is very much about finding balance in your life. Examples include balancing how much you study for individual classes, how much time you spend socially or in the library, or making sure you eat a balanced diet. Balancing communication with family and old friends is no different. Some students text or chat with their families or friends multiple times daily, while others do so every few days, once per week, or sometimes less often. What is important is that you figure out what is healthy and productive for you.

There are students who focus all of their social attention on previous relationships and never give themselves a chance to connect with all of the opportunities that the college environment provides. If your college or university is close to home, it can be tempting to keep hanging out with friends from high school and continuing your old high school habits. It is not to say that continuing old habits is a bad thing, they got you to college after all, but sometimes the relationships we form when young are more based on convenience and not fit. You should consider if some of those relationships are conducive to your college goals, or not. You may have old friends who are a lot of fun and that you love hanging out with, but sometimes the fun becomes too much or too often. Chapter 6 will take a deeper dive in to relationship management, including building your emotional network and learning to say "no."

As you get older it is natural that relationships fade, which can be sad, but also can be important for personal growth and new beginnings. Having to tell friends and family that you cannot be on the phone or social media with them all of the time, or attend every function can be difficult. Boundaries are important for everyone, and you may need to set some new boundaries with the major life change you are experiencing. If you have old friends or family that you are communicating with to a point where it is distracting you from achieving goals in college, make a plan for communicating with them. If they truly love and support you, they will understand diminished interactions. If not, you may need to consider letting go of some of those relationships.

## DISCOVERY

1. Consider some of your relationships with family and friends that take up much of your time. Are they conducive to your college success or presenting barriers to your college success in terms of time or emotional impact?

   _____

   _____

   _____

"The best piece of advice that I could give to a student just starting the semester would be that they immediately look at all of their syllabi. My favorite thing to do is take all of the due dates for assignments from the syllabus and transfer them over to my big wall calendar. This is how I stay organized. I find it helpful to be able to look at everything at once. Another piece of advice would be to really get to know your professors. I was always told that the closer you sit to the front of the class the more it shows your professor that you care more and makes you stand out to them as a student. Talking to your professor after the first class can be super beneficial, especially if you try to be consistent about going to ask them questions and be a proactive learner."

— Jordan S., senior, Public Health

## The College Syllabus

In your previous educational experience you probably had teachers or instructors who handed out a syllabus at the beginning of the term. You can expect each of your college classes to also have a syllabus as most colleges and universities require that their faculty provide a syllabus as a guide to students enrolled in the class.

In college, your course syllabus serves as a guide and contract for that class, and knowing how to navigate it is essential to your success. Your college professors will expect you to know the syllabus and use it as a resource for course policy, procedures, expectations, and schedule. College professors may not be willing to answer questions that can be answered by reading the syllabus. In fact, if you email them questions you could have answered yourself by reading the syllabus, their response may simply be "check the syllabus." Below are some items to look for on your college syllabi, as well as some tips that will help set a foundation for success in your classes:

- **Professor information.** Most syllabi include instructor contact information, including how best to contact them as well as office hours and location. Use your professor's contact information to reach out when your question cannot be answered by the syllabus.

- **Course description and objectives.** You will find a general statement describing what the course will cover, as well as learning objectives or goals for what you can expect to learn in the class (and what you will be expected to learn). This statement helps you better understand what to expect from the course, and whether the course is right for you and matches your goals and expectations as well.

- **Course format.** Format refers the medium in which the course is delivered (i.e., online, face to face, hybrid), as well as how information will be delivered in class (i.e., lectures, group collaboration, projects). The format may also be important to you in selecting the class, and in how you will prepare for it on a day-to-day basis.

- **Required materials, including textbook information.** You may find textbooks can be purchased or rented, or accessed online. In any case, get your textbooks, and get them early! You may be tempted to wait until classes begin to see if you can avoid purchasing a textbook, but if you do, you put yourself at risk of falling behind right away, as textbooks can run out of stock by the start of term! You may also be required to acquire other materials such as notebooks or binders, or more specialized items like course packets, subscriptions, or technology software or hardware.

- **Attendance and participation policy.** Some of your classes will require attendance, while others may not. It is important that you know the policy, and how nonattendance will impact your ability to pass. This will also likely include communication procedures if you do have to miss a class.

- **Assignments and grading.** Your assignments will be included in your syllabi or course schedules, as well as the weight of each on your final grade. Pay attention to the relative weights of various assignments and tests on your grade. While doing well on all assignments should always be the goal, it is not uncommon for students to focus primarily on assignments that count more in the final grade. While that may seem like a smart strategy, the smaller assignments such as daily participation, homework, or quizzes can add up quickly and should not be taken lightly.

- **Course policies or expectations.** These can include how to submit assignments, late work policy, classroom behavior expectations, and others. You should know how to submit assignments in each of your classes, and expect there to be some differences from class to class. Many professors expect an electronic or online submission that could be through a course website or other online space, though some may still ask students to bring paper versions to class. Submitting assignments incorrectly will likely result in either diminished credit or no credit at all.

- **Calendar or schedule.** Some professors will offer precise dates and times of class topics and assignment due dates, while others may be more vague. If you are fortunate to have precise due dates you should keep those dates in a place where you can refer to them easily and often so that they don't get lost in the shuffle.

While individual syllabi will vary, always remember that your course syllabi are your *first* resource for success in your classes. Get in the habit of keeping all of your syllabi each academic term in a place where you can refer to them easily and often. Some students keep them in a folder on their desk, while others hang them on the fridge! Do what it takes to make sure you have them when you need them.

"One of the most exciting things about being a new college student can be diving into your college culture and finding that you have lots of freedom and time to use as you wish! That was my own experience as a college student, and is something my college students have shared with me consistently over the past 25 years. They have also shared with me how important time management is for them. If there is one simple thing that can make your life better – both in college and in your career – it is to take control of your time. Sometimes this looks like choosing to enjoy a free afternoon with friends or family, and sometimes this looks like planning well in advance to study for a test. Though it can feel painful to spend time doing something you don't exactly enjoy, the pain of not doing well academically can be worse, and can significantly increase your stress and anxiety in the long run. Challenge yourself to be in charge of how you use your time."

— Dr. Jennifer Roth-Burnette

## Time Management and Your Study Plan ⊛

When we ask successful students what they consider one of the most important contributors to their success, *and* what they think struggling students have the most difficulty with, the answer is almost always the same: *time management.*

Our students share that for most classes, success is a matter of investing adequate time in study, as well as planning ahead for tests and large assignments or projects. A strong time management strategy includes identifying and eliminating time-wasters, using to-do lists, establishing routines, planning time for study and social engagements, and taking time off.

How do you use your time? Think back over the past 24 hours and consider how you spent each hour of the day. Did you spend time reading class materials, studying your notes, solving problems, working at a job, interacting with family or friends, working out, relaxing, checking social media, texting or answering calls, or surfing the internet?

> *Take the Time Tracker Challenge in the end-of-chapter activities! Find out how you are spending your time by tracking the next 24 hours. You may be surprised at your results!*

Be aware of how you spend your time.  This is the first step toward good time management. Once you know how you are spending your time, you can make intentional decisions about how to spend it, going forward. It is especially important to identify ways in which you may be wasting your time. Many students find that hours can simply disappear while checking social media, texting, and surfing the internet. While it is very important to keep up with friends and family, we encourage you to do so during break times that you identify. Checking social media or texting while trying to study can make your study less effective, because your mind is pulled in many different directions instead of being focused on the material you are studying.

**Avoid distractions.** Most people are not as good at multitasking as they think. Anything that distracts you from uninterrupted study will likely cause you difficulty in focusing to learn the material, making your study time longer. We recommend turning off videos, games, television and other distractions during your study time. Several of our students have shared that they use apps, such as Offtime and Flipd to shut down notifications from their phones while they are studying, to eliminate those distractions and stay focused. If you have difficulty staying off social media or messaging during your study time, consider looking for an app that could help you with that.

**Make a to-do list.** Listing your daily tasks is an essential practice that successful students use to organize their lives and ensure they are completing necessary tasks. Your to-do list can include everything you need to do in a given day, including personal tasks, study and reading, errands, and reminders. Once you have made your list for the day, if you are having difficulty getting started, begin with the smallest or easiest tasks. Getting something done and checking it off will help you build momentum for the more difficult tasks. As you continue checking off completed tasks, your momentum will build further.

As you move through your to-do list, be sure you are doing just one thing at a time. Multitasking can actually make you less productive, and make your tasks take longer than they have to. As you go through your day and become aware of additional things that need to be done, you can add them to today's list if they truly need to happen today, or use them to start making your list for tomorrow.

# To Do List

*© Darride/Shutterstock.com*

**Establish a routine** that helps you accomplish the things you need to do. Is your residence quiet in the mornings? You might want to use that time daily to study or read materials for class. Do you have a long break between two classes? That might be a good time to go to the library or find another quiet spot to study. Identify the blocks of time around your classes and your other obligations (like a job or family) that will be the best times for you to study, workout, socialize, and take care of personal needs. The more you stay with a routine, the less you will have to think about when you will accomplish the tasks you need to complete that day.

© NicoElNino/Shutterstock.com

Use a planner to plan your study time, in addition to your class schedule, social events, organization meetings, and the like. We recommend using a month-view calendar for an overall look at your month, and a weekly planner for your weekly schedule. You might wish to use a monthly wall calendar, for instance, and keep a notebook-style weekly planner. Or, you might identify a notebook-style planner that combines both styles, with a month-view at the beginning of each month and weekly planning pages for each week. If you feel you are likely to forget your planner in your backpack or your room, you may be better served by a digital calendar or planner.

> *We have provided templates for monthly and weekly planners at the end of this chapter. Feel free to tear those out and use them, or make copies of them for future use.*

Physical and digital planners have their pros and cons, so you should choose the one that best suits you, personally. If you choose a physical planner, know that the kinesthetic action of writing down your schedule and your obligations can help you remember your schedule more firmly. The same is true of your handwritten to-do list. If you are using a digital planner, you can take advantage of alarms and reminders to help you remember what you need to be doing.

Whichever style planner you choose, note down deadlines as soon as you know about them, and make checking your planner a part of your daily routine. These are the items you will want to note in your planner, to begin with:

- Your class meeting times
- Study time
- Personal and social obligations
- Self-care such as exercise, nutrition, and time for rest

**A note about study time:** Study includes reading assigned materials and/or watching assigned videos before class, reviewing notes after class, learning and understanding the material, completing homework assignments, and preparing for tests or larger projects. You should plan to study 2 to 3 hours for every hour you spend in class. In other words, if you are enrolled in a 3-credit-hour class that meets three hours per week total, then you should plan to study 6 to 9 hours per week for that class, depending on the difficulty of the material. If you are enrolled in 12 credit hours total, you should assume that you will need to dedicate 24 to 36 hours per week to study, both to prepare for class and to review after class, and to complete any additional assignments and prepare for tests.

| Enrolled in | Class meetings | Study time |
| --- | --- | --- |
| 3 credit hours | 2.5–3 hours per week | 6–9 hours per week |
| 12 credit hours | 10–12 hours per week | 24–36 hours per week |
| 15 credit hours | 13–15 hours per week | 30–45 hours per week |

## DISCOVERY

Use the chart above as an example for your own academic term:

| I am enrolled in | My classes meet a total of | I need to study |
| --- | --- | --- |
| _____ credit hours | _____ hours per week | _____ hours per week (meeting hours × 2 or 3) |

**Take time off daily and weekly.**  Long chunks of time spent working on assignments, reading and studying should be broken up with time away. Your mind and your senses need periodic breaks. During your study sessions, be sure to look away from the screen or physical text from time to time, and get up and move around at least once per hour to keep your body active. A 5- to 10-minute break each hour can help you focus better over a longer period of time. At least once per week, take a day or part of a day to relax, rest, and do something you enjoy. This decompression time is essential to balance and manage the feelings of stress and pressure that can crop up when you are working hard to study for challenging college classes.

"The best advice that I can give is to get a planner, you'll hear this almost every day of your freshman year and during orientation, but it is extremely helpful and beneficial. Once classes get close to beginning, professors will usually release their syllabus online. I would suggest you go through each of your syllabi and write down any exam dates, assignment due dates, and projects/presentations in your planner. That way you have a good idea of when things will be due and which weeks of the semester will be your busiest so you can plan accordingly and get ahead. Another piece of advice is to introduce yourself to your professor after the first class. This way they can put a name to a face and will recognize you when you go to their office hours or email for help. It also can come in handy down the road for letters of recommendation and things of that nature."

— Cody H., senior, Aerospace Engineering

"My biggest advice to first year students would be to get a calendar/planner, either one that can be easily seen such as a white board beside their beds or an online app that send reminders at every time interval or a paper back that they are certain that they will check. It is very easy to think you have it all figured out and you don't need a reminder, but it also happens that we have bad days or unscheduled events happen that could make you forget about an important exam. For the first week, go through the syllabus. The syllabus shows how strict or flexible the professor is and how the class will go. Most professors already have assignment deadlines and test dates and times in the syllabus so mark them all down and keep notes to plan ahead."

— Oreoluwa A., senior, Chemical Engineering

## A Basic Success Plan

In later chapters, you will learn specific strategies and methods for reading college texts, taking good notes, understanding how you learn, identifying your learning preferences, communicating with your professors, and the like. For the moment, here is a basic plan for success to get you off to a strong start.

A basic success plan in each class will include these elements:

1. Read assigned materials (watch assigned videos, listen to assigned lectures, etc.) *before* class. Take notes on these materials as you go through them.

2. Take notes *during* class.

3. Review notes *after* class.

4. Complete and submit assignments *by deadlines.*

## Figure 1.1:    Basic Success Plan.

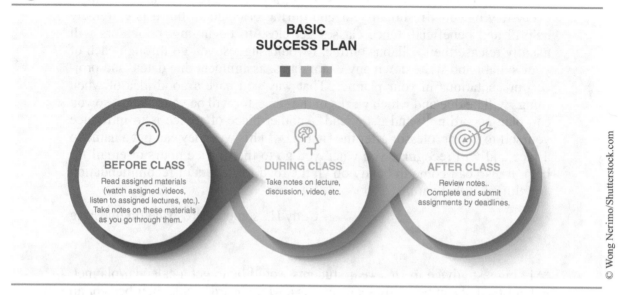

In order to complete this cycle, you need to **attend every class**. Think of your class time as a budget. If there are 30 class meetings in your academic term and you miss 6 of them, you have missed 20% of the class material. What are the chances you can do as well as you want to with 20% missed? What if you missed class half the time? How well would you do with 50% missed? Would you want to cut your financial spending budget by 20% or 50%? Think about whether you want to cut your knowledge budget by that much.

Make it a habit to attend every class to maintain your knowledge budget at 100%. Then, if a serious illness or true emergency causes you to miss a class, it will not negatively impact you as badly as if you had already missed several class meetings.

Complete the success plan outlined above for each class (before, during, and after), dedicate the time it takes to do so, and you will be well on your way to a successful academic term.

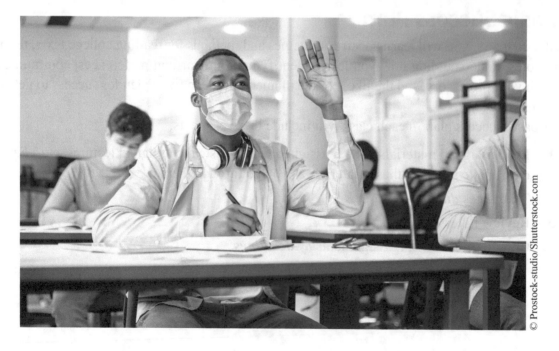

# Student Conduct and Civility

During your college orientation, and likely a few times thereafter, you have probably heard about your college or university's expectations for student behavior, or code of conduct. Your college or university's Student Code of Conduct may be presented in many forms, such as a "creed" or ways the institution expects students to present themselves, or as a book or rules and consequences for those who don't follow them. Codes of conduct often include expectations for the treatment of others, for behavior inside and outside of the classroom, for diversity, equity, and inclusion, and for other types of civilized behavior. It is important that you have a general understanding of your college or university's code of conduct so that you can understand how to be a successful member of the campus community and culture. You need to understand expected behaviors, but also know the consequences of code violation. If you are unfamiliar with your college or university's code of conduct, it is in your best interest to check it out.

## Discovery

1. Locate your college or university's code of conduct. What are some of the main points or sections included in the code?

   _____

   _____

   _____

2. Based on what you discovered in the code, what do you think the main points can tell you about the culture of your college or university?

   _____

   _____

   _____

3. Identify at least 2 items that you learned from exploring your college or university's code of conduct.

   _____

   _____

   _____

Most students have a general understanding of what civilized or civil behavior is, and are unlikely to be confronted by the negative consequences of a student conduct code. Simply put, civility is exhibiting behaviors for the social advancement defined by a civilization, community, or other organization. While civility can differentiate among communities, most experts agree it has to do with courtesy, politeness, good manners, and the awareness of the rights, wishes, and feelings of others. Another way civility can be explained in simplistic terms is by the Golden Rule: treating others as you would like to be treated.

On college and university campuses, there are many opportunities for students to not be civil (or practice incivility) toward others. Rehling and Bjorklund (2010) characterize classroom incivility as "contrary to the well-being of the classroom community, including behaviors that distract the instructor or other students, disrupt classroom learning, discourage the instructor from teaching, discourage other students from participating, and derail the instructor's goals for the period." Just because you aren't confronted with consequences of the Student Conduct Code, doesn't mean you haven't exhibited behaviors that can be considered in-civil. Below are some common examples of incivility inside the classroom:

- Sleeping in class
- Disapproving groans, sighs, or gestures
- Acting disinterested or bored
- Not attending class or arriving late
- On your mobile device
- Regularly leaving during class
- Dominating group work or a class discussion
- Not participating or completing readings or homework
- Not having materials that you need, including the course textbook
- Cheating or plagiarism
- Not turning in assignments as indicated in syllabus

While most of these examples of incivility are relatively minor, they can have a profound effect on others, and may have immediate or long-term consequences for you. It goes without saying that incivility also occurs outside of the classroom, below are examples:

- Littering
- Not keeping living, eating, or work areas clean
- Bullying, intimidation, or harassment on social media or elsewhere
- Underage drinking or other substance abuse
- Being late or not showing up for appointments with faculty or staff
- Not following published procedures in general (e.g., not making advising appointments when invited, missing deadlines)

## DISCOVERY

1. For the above examples of incivility, circle the examples that you have witnessed others do so far this semester.
2. For the above examples, **underline** the examples that you have done yourself this semester.
3. List other examples of incivility you have witnessed that are not mentioned above.

_____

_____

_____

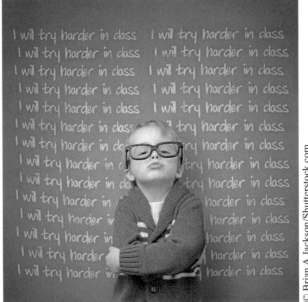

## Getting Involved with Student Life Early and Responsibly

During your orientation to your college or university you will be (or were already) bombarded with many fun and exciting ways to get involved with the university and your new peers. You should take advantage of the first few weeks you are on campus to explore opportunities for making friends, having fun, and getting involved in organizations such as fraternities and sororities, clubs and organizations, athletic events, and other events and social experiences. However, you should also remember that your college experience is not a sprint, but instead a marathon of opportunity. You need to pace yourself. Be careful not to overextend yourself right away, and make sure you set aside time for classes and responsibilities that go along with starting off on the correct foot and achieving early academic success.

## Creating a Living Space Agreement with Your New Roommate ⊖

Most college students living on campus have roommates, whether they are roommates within a suite with separate sleeping areas, or sleeping in the same room. If your living situation prior to college required you to share space with a sibling, you are at an advantage. Whether you realize it or not, through that experience you learned at least some compromise and patience. If you are sharing living space with someone for the first time when you come to college, you may need to develop some of these skills, and do so quickly.

Nowadays, colleges and universities connect roommates with each other prior to their arrival which allows coordination of who is bringing what to the shared space, but also can help set the foundation for the relationship by getting to know one another early. Although this is beneficial, differences in personalities, habits, and the stressors that arise can cause conflict between roommates. Especially if you do not know your roommates prior to arrival at college, you can at times anticipate at least some level of disagreement in terms of space cleanliness, quiet times, sharing of property, and guests to the room. Even if you and your roommates are the best of friends from high school, you are still likely to have disagreements at least part of the time. A way to be proactive in avoiding surprises from or disagreements with your roommates is completing a roommate agreement during your first week living together. A roommate agreement, or guidelines for the shared space developed among roommates is not only helpful for setting boundaries and guidelines for your living space, but will also provide an early opportunity to get to know your roommates more deeply, and developing a cooperative relationship.

Some colleges provide roommate agreements for navigating these common challenges. Whether your college or university provides one or not, you should strongly consider it. At the end of this chapter, you will find an example roommate agreement you can use.

## Chapter Summary

This chapter has provided you with a variety of concepts and resources that will help you "set the tone" for college success, but this is just the beginning! Now that you have been introduced to the grit concept, gained some tips for what to bring to college and what to leave behind, and navigate your syllabi, it is time to put these concepts in to action. The rest of this book will take a deeper dive some of these same concepts, but also introduce you to many new ones. Once you identify what your "college success" is, begin making choices to achieve it, today. Good luck on your journey!

## End-of-Chapter Activities

I.  **Syllabus Analysis Activity.** For each of your college syllabi, answer the following questions:

1.  What is the name of the faculty teaching this course?

    _____

2.  What is the best way to contact the faculty person?

    _____

3.  Where and when can I attend office hours?

    _____

4.  What textbooks or other materials do I need for this class?

    _____

5.  What is this class about? What can I expect to learn?

    _____

6.  On what basis will my learning be assessed in this class? (tests, assignments, participation, other?)

    _____

    a.  What activities or requirements count the most toward my grade?

        _____

    b.  Are there daily or weekly activities that will add up over time?

        _____

    c.  What else stands out to me about how my grade will be determined?

        _____

7.  When are the major test dates and assignment deadlines in this class?

    _____

8.  Are there weekly assignments or homework that I will need to turn in regularly?

    _____

9.  What is the attendance policy for this class? What should I do if I have to miss a class?

    _____

**II. Time Tracker Activity.** With this activity, you will discover how you spend your time each week to determine how well you balance your time.

First, estimate the number of hours you spend on the following activities

Sleeping each night _____ × 7 = _____

Showering/preparing for the day _____ × 7 = _____

Eating each day _____ × 7 = _____

Commuting (driving, walking, etc.) each day _____ × 7 = _____

Watching TV, gaming, social media, videos each day _____ × 7 = _____

Socializing with friends each day (hanging/going out) _____ × 7 = _____

Regular activities per week (meetings, working out, etc.) _____

Working a job per week _____

In class per week _____

General relaxing and other miscellaneous activities per week _____

Total: _____

Now, subtract your hour total from 168, the total number of hours in a week. That will show you how many hours you have remaining in the week to spend on homework and study.

168 hours in a week

− _____ total hours above

= _____ hours left to study

Based on what you learned earlier in Chapter 1, do you have enough time each week left to study and achieve your goals? If not, take a hard look at what you currently spend time on that you can cut. Remember that balance is important, so don't cut out all social or relaxation activities, begin with time-wasters you spend a lot of time on that may include TV, social media, gaming, or going out.

III. **Monthly Planners.** Complete the following fill-in monthly planner pages for the entirety of your academic term, or use your own monthly calendar (printed or digital).

    a. Fill in month-names and dates for each month

    b. Using your college's academic calendar, fill in the beginning and end of term, study week and exam week, and any breaks or holidays.

    c. Using your syllabus, fill in important assignment deadlines and test dates for each class you are taking.

    d. Using your college's events calendar, fill in upcoming events that you don't want to miss.

    e. Fill in any other date-specific items you want to be sure not to miss (like tryouts for intramural sports, a kickboxing class you wanted to take, or upcoming concerts).

    f. Make a habit of consulting your calendar on a daily basis.

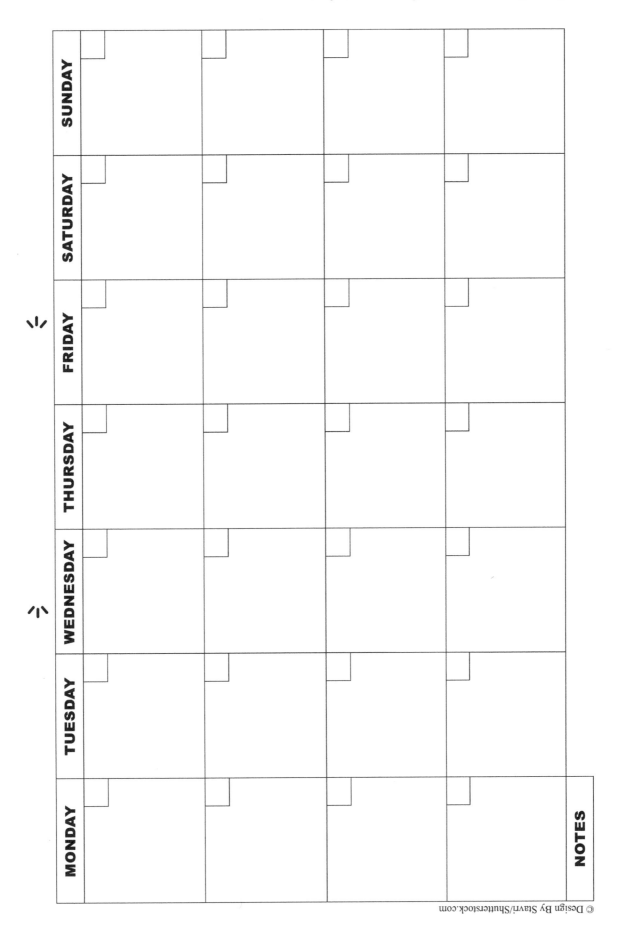

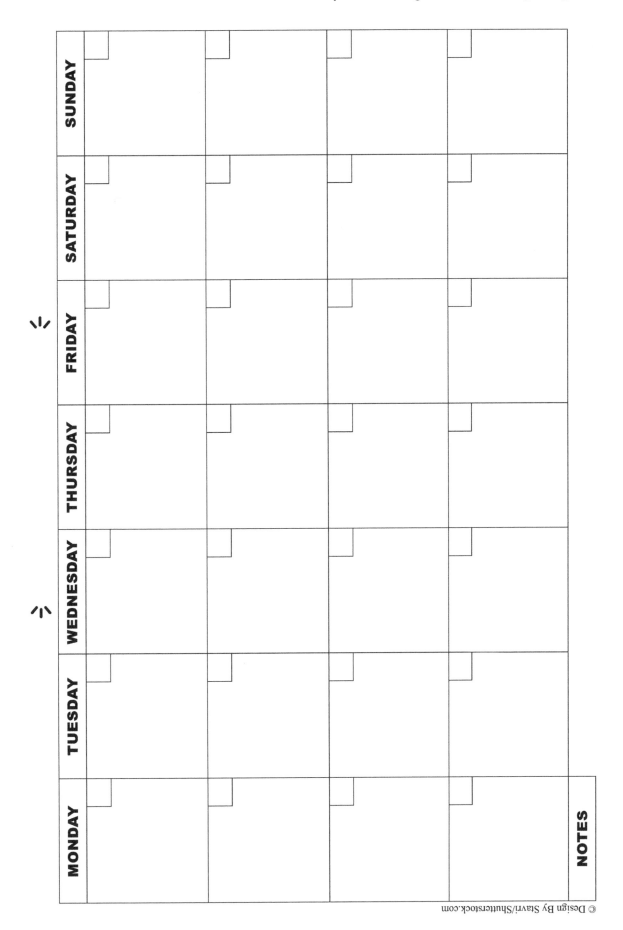

| MONDAY | TUESDAY | WEDNESDAY | THURSDAY | FRIDAY | SATURDAY | SUNDAY |
|---|---|---|---|---|---|---|
| | | | | | | |
| | | | | | | |
| | | | | | | |
| NOTES | | | | | | |

| MONDAY | TUESDAY | WEDNESDAY | THURSDAY | FRIDAY | SATURDAY | SUNDAY |
|---|---|---|---|---|---|---|
| | | | | | | |
| | | | | | | |
| | | | | | | |
| | | | | | | |

**NOTES**

| MONDAY | TUESDAY | WEDNESDAY | THURSDAY | FRIDAY | SATURDAY | SUNDAY |
|---|---|---|---|---|---|---|
| | | | | | | |
| | | | | | | |
| | | | | | | |
| | | | | | | |
| **NOTES** | | | | | | |

**IV. Weekly Planners.** Complete the following fill-in weekly planner page for the next week, or use your own planner (printed or digital).

    **a.** Fill in meeting times for your classes and labs.

    **b.** Fill in your organizational meetings, work hours, and other important obligations.

    **c.** Considering how much time you need to study (which you determined on page 49), fill in your study hours for the week. Try to arrange them in a way that will allow you at least an afternoon and evening off once per week.

    **d.** Note whether any of the days for the coming week have important events that you need to make time for. Adjust your planner as needed.

    **e.** Make a habit of consulting your planner on a daily basis.

## WEEKLY PLANNER

| | MONDAY | TUESDAY | WEDNESDAY | THURSDAY | FRIDAY | SATURDAY | SUNDAY |
|---|---|---|---|---|---|---|---|
| 8:00 am | | | | | | | |
| 9:00 am | | | | | | | |
| 10:00 am | | | | | | | |
| 11:00 am | | | | | | | |
| 12:00 pm | | | | | | | |
| 1:00 pm | | | | | | | |
| 2:00 pm | | | | | | | |
| 3:00 pm | | | | | | | |
| 4:00 pm | | | | | | | |
| 5:00 pm | | | | | | | |
| 6:00 pm | | | | | | | |
| 7:00 pm | | | | | | | |
| 8:00 pm | | | | | | | |
| 9:00 pm | | | | | | | |
| 10:00 pm | | | | | | | |

## WEEKLY PLANNER

| | MONDAY | TUESDAY | WEDNESDAY | THURSDAY | FRIDAY | SATURDAY | SUNDAY |
|---|---|---|---|---|---|---|---|
| 8:00 am | | | | | | | |
| 9:00 am | | | | | | | |
| 10:00 am | | | | | | | |
| 11:00 am | | | | | | | |
| 12:00 pm | | | | | | | |
| 1:00 pm | | | | | | | |
| 2:00 pm | | | | | | | |
| 3:00 pm | | | | | | | |
| 4:00 pm | | | | | | | |
| 5:00 pm | | | | | | | |
| 6:00 pm | | | | | | | |
| 7:00 pm | | | | | | | |
| 8:00 pm | | | | | | | |
| 9:00 pm | | | | | | | |
| 10:00 pm | | | | | | | |

# WEEKLY PLANNER

| | MONDAY | TUESDAY | WEDNESDAY | THURSDAY | FRIDAY | SATURDAY | SUNDAY |
|---|---|---|---|---|---|---|---|
| 8:00 am | | | | | | | |
| 9:00 am | | | | | | | |
| 10:00 am | | | | | | | |
| 11:00 am | | | | | | | |
| 12:00 pm | | | | | | | |
| 1:00 pm | | | | | | | |
| 2:00 pm | | | | | | | |
| 3:00 pm | | | | | | | |
| 4:00 pm | | | | | | | |
| 5:00 pm | | | | | | | |
| 6:00 pm | | | | | | | |
| 7:00 pm | | | | | | | |
| 8:00 pm | | | | | | | |
| 9:00 pm | | | | | | | |
| 10:00 pm | | | | | | | |

# WEEKLY PLANNER

| | MONDAY | TUESDAY | WEDNESDAY | THURSDAY | FRIDAY | SATURDAY | SUNDAY |
|---|---|---|---|---|---|---|---|
| 8:00 am | | | | | | | |
| 9:00 am | | | | | | | |
| 10:00 am | | | | | | | |
| 11:00 am | | | | | | | |
| 12:00 pm | | | | | | | |
| 1:00 pm | | | | | | | |
| 2:00 pm | | | | | | | |
| 3:00 pm | | | | | | | |
| 4:00 pm | | | | | | | |
| 5:00 pm | | | | | | | |
| 6:00 pm | | | | | | | |
| 7:00 pm | | | | | | | |
| 8:00 pm | | | | | | | |
| 9:00 pm | | | | | | | |
| 10:00 pm | | | | | | | |

**V. Roommate Agreement.** Below is a roommate agreement template. It might be a good idea to complete with your roommates early when you move in together to avoid future disagreements.

---

# Roommate Agreement Template

All roommates agree to the terms and will share the responsibilities outlined below.

Roommates

1. _____

2. _____

3. _____

4. _____

This agreement is active from _____ to _____

• • • • • • • • • • • • • • • • • • • • • • • • • • • • • • • • • • • • • • • • • • • • • • • •

Study Times: The room/suite is required to be free from noise (e.g., TV, music, social)

Monday:   from ____ to ____      Tuesday: from ____ to ____      Wednesday: from ____ to ____

Thursday: from ____ to ____      Friday:   from ____ to ____      Saturday:   from ____ to ____

Sunday:   from ____ to ____

• • • • • • • • • • • • • • • • • • • • • • • • • • • • • • • • • • • • • • • • • • • • • • • •

Sleep Times: The room/suite is required to be free from noise

Monday:   from ____ to ____      Tuesday: from ____ to ____      Wednesday: from ____ to ____

Thursday: from ____ to ____      Friday:   from ____ to ____      Saturday:   from ____ to ____

Sunday:   from ____ to ____

• • • • • • • • • • • • • • • • • • • • • • • • • • • • • • • • • • • • • • • • • • • • • • • •

Borrowing Items

The following items CANNOT be borrowed: _____

_____

The following items CAN be borrowed WITH PERMISSION: _____

_____

The following items CAN be borrowed WITHOUT PERMISSION: _____

_____

• • • • • • • • • • • • • • • • • • • • • • • • • • • • • • • • • • • • • • • • • • • • • • • •

Cleaning: Cleaning of shared space in the room/suite should be done weekly. Roommates can ____ share tasks each week, or ____ a single roommate do all tasks for assigned weeks.

Consistent day room should be cleaned: ☐ MON   ☐ TUE   ☐ WED   ☐ THU   ☐ FRI   ☐ SAT   ☐ SUN

Tasks (initial each task if assigning tasks to individual roommate for each week):

——— sweep/vacuum    ——— dishes    ——— take out trash    ——— wipe surfaces    ——— toilets

——— wipe sinks    ——— clean shower    ——— other: _____

——— other: _____    ——— other: _____

**Cleaning Costs:** Each roommate will provide $_____ weekly / monthly / yearly for cleaning supplies.

• • • • • • • • • • • • • • • • • • • • • • • • • • • • • • • • • • • • • • • • • • • • • • • • •

**Overnight Guests:** ☐ Not allowed    ☐ Allowed with permission    ☐ Allowed without permission

Other points of interest: _____
_____
_____
_____
_____

By signing below each roommate acknowledges and agrees to the terms of this agreement.

| | | |
|---|---|---|
| Printed Name | Signature | Date |
| Printed Name | Signature | Date |
| Printed Name | Signature | Date |
| Printed Name | Signature | Date |

# References

Downing, S. (2017). *On course: Strategies for creating success in college and in life. Study skills plus* (3rd ed.). Cengage Learning.

Forni, P. M. (2002). *Choosing civility: The twenty-five rules of considerate conduct.* St. Martin's Griffin.

Rehling, D. L., & Bjorklund, W. L. (2010). A comparison of faculty and student perceptions of incivility in the classroom. *Journal on Excellence in College Teaching, 21*(3), 73–93.

Weeks, K. M. (2011). *In search of civility: Confronting incivility on the college campus.* Morgan James Publishing.

Baldwin, A., Bunting, B., Daugherty, D., Lewis, L., & Steenbergh, T. (2020). *Promoting belonging, growth mindset, and resilience to foster student success.* National Resource Center for The First-Year Experience.

Barbouta, A., Barbouta, C., & Kotrotsiou, S. (2020). Growth mindset and grit: How do university students' mindsets and grit affect their academic achievement? *International Journal of Caring Sciences, 13*(1), 654–664.

Choroszy, M., N., & Meek, T. M. (2020). *Success for all: Programs to support students throughout their college experience.* University of Nevada Press.

Duckworth, A. (2016). *Grit: The power of passion and perseverance.* Scribner.

Grant, M. (December 2006). Will Smith Interview: "Will Power: One Driven Guy." *Reader's Digest*, 88–95.

Hoerr, T. R. (2017). *The formative five: Fostering grit, empathy, and other success skills every student needs.* ASCD.

Hoerr, T. R., & Baruch-Feldman, C. (2017). *The grit guide for teens: A workbook to help you build perseverance, self-control, and a growth mindset.* Instant Help.

King's College. (2021). *How is college different from high school?* https://www.kings.edu/admissions/hs_sophomores_and_juniors/preparing_for_college/high_school_vs_college

Pelletier, K. (2019). Student success: 3 big questions. *Educause Review.* https://er.educause.edu/articles/2019/10/student-success-3-big-questions

Purdue University Global. (2018). *Time management tips for busy college students.* https://www.purdueglobal.edu/blog/student-life/time-management-busy-college-students/

Roberson, S. (2020). Developing student success through persistence: Teaching more than content. *Education, 141*(2), 83–100.

Sherman, M. C. (2019). In their own words: A phenomenological exploration of student mental health and success in college. *Social Work Research, 43*(3), 145–156. https://doi.org/10.1093/swr/svz006

Terrell, L. S. (2019). *College students' sense of belonging: A key to educational success for all students* (2nd ed.). Routledge.

## Chapter 2

# Foundations for Success

| Choices of Successful Students | Choices of Struggling Students |
|---|---|
| 1. Learn the basic organizational structure of their college or university. | 1. Ignore college or university organizational structure and have difficulty finding resources and can feel lost or frustrated. |
| 2. Find ways of getting involved in their college's culture. | 2. Fail to engage in the college culture and feel disconnected, alone, or homesick. |
| 3. Learn common college or university vocabulary. | 3. Are often confused by college vocabulary and miss out on opportunities and deadlines. |
| 4. Communicate proactively with their faculty. | 4. Do not communicate with faculty. |
| 5. Proactively address what might put their college success at risk. | 5. Do not prepare for personal roadblocks and are often challenged by them. |
| 6. Ask questions about what they are learning. | 6. Learn passively, and as a result don't learn much at all. |
| 7. Find ways to make learning social. | 7. Fail to make connections with others in their classes. |
| 8. Take healthy steps to alleviate stress. | 8. De-stress in unhealthy or unproductive ways that only work temporarily. |
| 9. Set SMART goals for study and academics. | 9. Passively set goals that hold no real value to them. |
| 10. Take good care of their physical, mental, and emotional health. | 10. Make choices detrimental to their physical, mental, and emotional health. |

© Prostock-studio/Shutterstock.com

# Introduction

Chapter 1 covered time-sensitive topics chosen to help you get off to a good start during your first couple weeks of the semester such as how to effectively manage your time and what to do before, during, and after each class. In Chapter 2 you will gain a "birds-eye" view of the college and university community, and how to fit into your new environment successfully. You will also learn how to activate your brain for learning, set effective goals, and practice good self-care to get you off to a solid start in studying for college classes and balancing your life.

## Focus Questions:

1. What is the Iceberg Model, and how does it relate to your self-perception?
2. What are common college and university structures, cultures, and vocabulary?
3. How can you activate your brain for learning in college?
4. What are common barriers to college success?

# The Iceberg Model of the Self

Did you know that icebergs are much larger than they appear? While 10% to 20% of an iceberg is visible above the surface of the ocean, that top portion or "tip of the iceberg" is very small compared to the 80% to 90% that supports it, below the water's surface.

© Romolo Tavani/Shutterstock.com

Several decades ago, researchers in the area of organizational management found that measures of raw intelligence could not accurately predict whether someone would be successful in their career on in achieving life goals. They found instead that *competencies*, or knowledge and skills related to those career and life goals, were the strongest indicators of future success. These researchers used an iceberg model to describe individual competencies, suggesting that while skills and knowledge represented the tip of the iceberg (or the 20% you can see), those skills and that knowledge were supported by a much larger set (the 80% you cannot see) of personal characteristics, experiences, values, hard work, and identities.

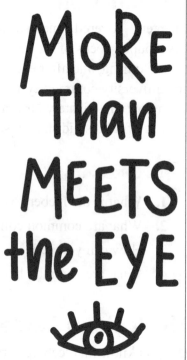

© YasnaTen/Shutterstock.com

By the same token, the "you" that you present to the world is just a small part of the total "you." While you probably present yourself in a way that shows what you want others to see – in how you dress, how you carry yourself, the words you use, and how you engage with others – there is much more about you than what appears on the surface. With icebergs, as with people, there is much more than meets the eye.

## DISCOVERY

1. How do I present myself to others? Write down three characteristics that you anticipate your professors and classmates can see about you right away, the first time they meet you.

   _____

   _____

   _____

2. Now, consider the things people will not know about you right away. Describe three things about you that are fundamental to who you are as a person (your character, your values, your identity) that you do not think people see right away.

   _____

   _____

   _____

The first characteristics you named, the elements of you that people see nearly immediately, can be compared to the tip of the iceberg. They form part of the 20% that is evident on the surface. The second set of characteristics you listed, those things that are fundamental to your sense of self but are typically not visible to others right away, form part of the 80% that is unseen. For people just as for icebergs, the 80% foundation – comprised of your character, your self-discipline, your values, your hard work and your identity – is absolutely essential to support the 20% or so that you share with the world.

"One invisible or below-the-surface element that I believe has created success in my academic career is being proactive. When I receive an assignment, I like to start early. Instead of doing it all at the last minute, I can split the assignment up into parts and work a little bit each day so I don't feel as crammed. Another element is connecting with classmates in my major specific classes. This way, I make friends and colleagues so later down the road if we have more classes together, it makes it easier to get together to study for an exam or work on assignments/projects. It also comes in handy because you never know if you'll end up working with these friends at the same institution or company."

— Cody H., senior, Aerospace Engineering

Your individual success can also be described as an iceberg, as in the diagram below. If your success (making good grades, achieving graduation, finding your dream job, meeting life goals) is the part that people see on the surface, keep in mind that there is much more beneath the surface, supporting your success, that people may not see: your persistence and sacrifice, your hard work and dedication, your good habits and disappointments, and even your failures. Remember, success is never 100% of the picture and is never 100% of the time. Success is built on determination and diligence. Every challenging experience (including failure!) can become a learning opportunity, and is part of the foundation from which you build future success.

## Figure 2.1: The Iceberg Model.

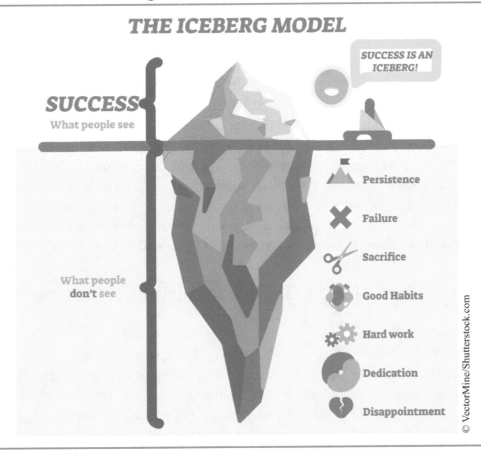

> **DISCOVERY**
>
> 1. In what ways have I already formed my character for success? Choose two "beneath the surface" attributes from the diagram above and describe how you are demonstrating those qualities during your first year of college.
>
>    _____
>
>    _____
>
>    _____
>
> 2. Now, choose one "beneath the surface" attribute that you see as a growing edge, or a quality you would like to cultivate further. Describe how you plan to cultivate that quality.
>
>    _____
>
>    _____
>
>    _____
>
> 3. How will the three qualities you listed above help you build toward your success?
>
>    _____
>
>    _____
>
>    _____

Why the iceberg? It reminds us that there is more to us than meets the eye, and that our character, values and hard work are fundamentally important to us as people as well as to our success in college, career, and life. The iceberg also reminds us as we meet new professors, advisors, classmates and friends that each person is their own iceberg of sorts – each person we meet is considerably more than meets the eye. And finally, college is its own iceberg, with much more going on beneath the surface and behind the scenes than is immediately apparent to many new college students. We encourage you to approach college with an open mind, aware that there is much more to learn about the many ways it can support you in your future endeavors. Arming yourself with knowledge, as you will do over the course of using this text, will help you make the most of your college experience, and increase your opportunities to make it a successful experience that you can shape in the ways that are most beneficial to you.

# University and College Organizational Structure

## Colleges vs. Universities

You likely have friends from high school who went to different universities, colleges, or even trade schools. Each of these are forms of postsecondary education (after high school). Colleges and universities are also considered institutions of higher education. Because of the nature of this workbook, you are most likely either already enrolled at a college or university, or are planning to. For that reason, this book will focus only on college and university structures.

Not all colleges and universities are the same, by a long shot. You could be reading this book on the campus of a large, public university with 50,000+ students, the campus of a small, private college with fewer than 1,000 students, a college you attend primarily online, or anything in between. Both colleges and universities offer degrees and/or professional training, can offer graduate (after 4-year or undergraduate/bachelor's degree) programs, can be in-person or online, and have athletics teams. Understanding some of the basics of college and university structure and cultures will help you navigate your campus.

The primary official difference between a college and university is that universities must have a certain number of accredited or officially recognized graduate programs for a designated length of time, that's really it. Unofficially, however, universities tend to have larger enrollment, have a wider array of graduate or professional degree options, and have a greater focus on faculty research than do colleges. Prestigious Ivy League institutions such as Harvard and Yale are universities, as are many state "flagship" universities such as The University of Alabama and The University of Illinois at Urbana-Champaign. There are also many public, regional serving universities such as Eastern Illinois University or Western Carolina University, or private universities such as Belmont University in Nashville or Maryville University in St. Louis. Colleges include 2-year community colleges, 4-year colleges, and a combination of the two. Community colleges are often open enrollment meaning any student with a high school diploma or equivalent living in the region can enroll. Colleges and universities typically have minimum admission requirements that often include subject specific requirements (e.g., English, math, and science), high school grade point average (GPA), standardized test scores (e.g., ACT or SAT), and others.

## Common College and University Organizational Structure

The internal structure of your college or university is determined by characteristics such as public or private, its age, size, or mission, to name a few, but will in general have a structure similar to that shown in Figure 2.2. Your university has a president or chancellor whose primary respon-sibility is securing a firm financial future for your institution. Most of the day-to-day responsi-bilities of the president are external, meeting with alumni, legislators, financial contributors, and community leaders. The president serves as the public "face" of the institution and clarifies the public image of the university, often appearing in the media or making speeches to the student body and public.

Reporting directly to the president in most large university organizational structures are executive vice presidents or just vice presidents who are in charge of their own large units within the college or university. The Academic Affairs unit (the vice president of Academic Affairs is commonly referred to as the Provost) typically houses the academic colleges or schools, as well as areas that promote academic endeavors such as research centers, libraries, and academic support offices such as tutoring and advising. Student Affairs (or Student Life) is another unit led by an executive vice president (the vice president of student affairs is commonly referred to as the Dean of Students). Student Affairs houses many of the nonacademic services such as residence life, health services, counseling centers, career services, student activities, athletics, and diversity/equity/inclusion centers. The enrollment management unit houses offices such as admissions, new student orientation, financial aid, and the university registrar, while the administration and finance unit houses business offices such as human resources, the bursar (student accounts or billing), campus police, food and dining, and facility operations. A final unit often found in a large university is external relations which often houses development and fundraising offices, alumni affairs, and community and government relations.

The vice presidents are responsible for their respective areas, and the university president relies on vice presidents for day-to-day operations within their units. In smaller colleges and universities some of these units or the offices within them are combined or do not exist at all.

## Figure 2.2:    Example Large University Organizational Structure.

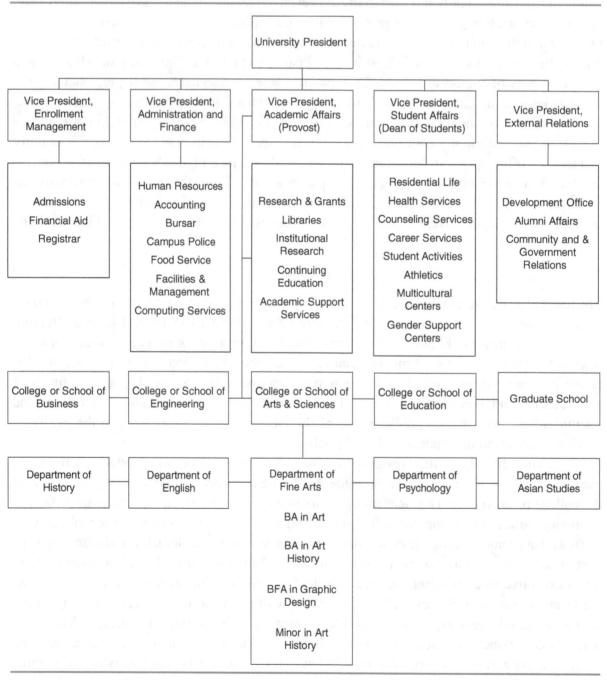

*Source*: Brian Gorman.

You will work with some of these offices directly as an undergraduate student, while others operate outside of undergraduate student needs. As you can see, college and university structures are complex. The offices most important to your success as a new college student will be discussed further in the "Student Services" section of Chapter 3.

The most important and largest divisions within Academic Affairs are the academic entities of the institution, often referred to as colleges, schools, or departments. Though the hierarchical structure and terminology are different from institution to institution, the general hierarchy is college – school – department (though sometimes colleges and schools are interchangeable, or sometimes 1 or 2 categories are missing completely). So, your university could also have colleges within it. If you go to a college that does not meet the aforementioned university requirement, you will likely see schools and departments and not academic colleges within the larger college. Common academic colleges include Arts and Sciences, Engineering, Business or Management, Education, or others. Common departments include English, History, or Psychology (College of Arts and Sciences), Economics, Accounting, Business (College of Business or Management), Electrical Engineering, Mechanical Engineering, Chemical or Biological Engineering (College of Engineering), Music Education, Special Education, Educational Leadership (College of Education). Departments house your academic major and minor.

---

### DISCOVERY

1. Am I enrolled in a college or university? How do I know?

   _____

   _____

   _____

2. How are my academic units organized? Does my college or university have colleges, departments, or both?

   _____

   _____

   _____

---

## College Cultures

### A Brief History of Higher Education in the United States

The history of your college or university may have a big impact on its culture. The first institutions of higher education in the American colonies were primarily established for the purpose of training community and colonial leadership. Early enrollment was small and selective with primarily only White, Christian, males allowed to attend and several who attended were framers of early colonial American government systems. Examples of early colonial institutions include Harvard, The College of New Jersey (now Princeton), and The College of William and Mary.

As Americans moved West and South, so did the establishment of more colleges that became known as frontier colleges as they were established on the rural frontier. These colleges also often served the purpose of educating local leaders, but also often had an expectation for training religious leaders to spread their word to Native American populations. Colonial colleges were most often privately funded and often by religious organizations. The British government saw the American colonies as a place for harvesting natural resources, not expanding education.

The mid-to-late 1800s saw a boom of establishments of colleges and universities, primarily as part of the Land-Grant College Act of 1862, commonly known as the Morrill Act. The Morrill Act of 1862, named after then Vermont Senator John Morrill, offered 30,000 acres of land per member of U.S. Congress for the purpose of establishing public colleges and universities that would focus on agriculture or mechanic arts such as engineering. Institutions with "A&M" in the title are examples of Morrill Act colleges, though most do not include "A&M" in their title. The Morrill Act of 1862 also provided funding for existing colleges and universities so long as they established agricultural colleges. This marked the first-time federal aid was provided for higher education and laid the foundation for a national system of colleges and universities. The Second Morrill Act of 1890 included a provision that disallowed racial discrimination under the Morrill Acts and extended funding and acreage opportunities for colleges for Black Americans. Today, 17 of the remaining Morrill Act of 1890 institutions are among the more than 100 Historically Black Colleges and Universities (HBCU) that exist today. In all, more than 100 million acres were allocated as a result of both Morrill Acts and brought higher education to millions of students.

## Figure 2.3:   Morrill Act Institutions of Contiguous United States (National Research Council, 1995).

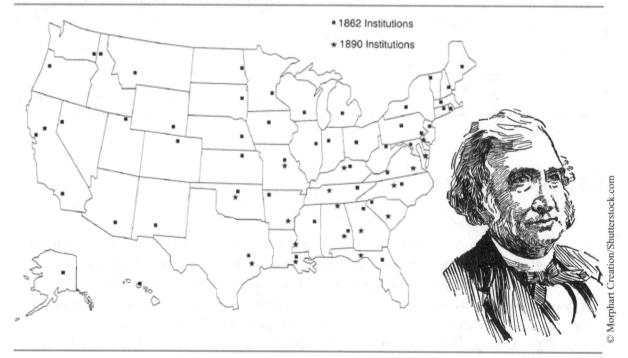

## Normal Schools

Another common way colleges and universities were initially established was for training students to be teachers so that they could educate children of the region. Prior to normal schools, the task of teaching elementary school students often went to clergymen or a willing and most deserving 8th grade graduate. The first public American "normal school" was established in Lexington, Vermont in 1839, with normal schools continuing to be developed into the early 20th century. By the 1930s normal schools had transitioned in to teachers colleges, and by the 1950s become departments within colleges or schools of education within state regional universities. Today it may be difficult to notice how college or university establishment as a normal school affect culture, though several still use it as a major part of their identity, especially through their education colleges and departments.

## Historically Black Colleges and Universities

Prior to the passing of the second Morrill Act in 1890, very few universities or "institutes" existed for the purpose of educating Black Americans and most services were only elementary and high school education, not postsecondary. Historically Black Colleges and Universities, commonly referred to as HBCUs, were established during the period of American legal segregation prior to the Civil Rights Act of 1964 to serve the postsecondary needs of Black Americans. In 2018, 292,000 students attended 101 HBCUs spread across 19 states, the District of Columbia, and the U.S. Virgin Islands. HBCUs have a rich tradition of social justice from a historical and contemporary perspective, and have produced major figures such as Medgar Evers (Alcorn State), Stokely Carmichael (Howard University), and Dr. Martin Luther King, Jr. (Morehouse College). HBCU curriculums are often rich in Black and continental African history and highly relevant to the identity development Black American student populations. The "HBCU experience" is known for embracing oral traditions, arts and language, mannerisms, family, and community ties.

## Tribal Colleges and Universities

Like HBCUs, Tribal Colleges and Universities (TCU) have been established to further the educational opportunities of an underserved ethnic group, this time for Native Americans. Most often located in the northern regions and Southwestern United States, the 32 TCUs in the U.S. have a collective unique culture of their own. Missions of TCUs are often culture-based, reflecting Indigenous values and beliefs throughout the curriculum, program offerings, and courses for the purpose preserving and honoring tribal culture. Indications are that it is working, as TCU students report that the focus on native language and culture improve self-image and confidence, as well as their abilities to understand, communicate, and interact with their tribes.

> *"I find it very important, not only to gain credit for the basic subjects such as math, science, and history, and the usual academic courses like that, but to actually learn about my own self-identity of my history, my ancestors' teachings, and the Navajo philosophy – TCU student (Preserving Culture, 2019, p. 3)."*

## Hispanic Serving Institutions

Hispanic Serving Institutions (HSI) are designations colleges and universities can gain if their enrollment is at least 25% Hispanic. Unlike HBCUs and TCUs that were established specifically for improving educational experiences of Black and Native Americans, colleges and universities can apply for HSI designation when their enrollment meets the required minimum. HSI designation provides opportunities for additional resources and funding from the federal government for qualifying institutions. As a result, missions of HSIs are less likely to include the celebration or preservation of a particular culture and instead be similar to predominately White institutions as described in the next section below. Some HSIs do not publish their HSI designation in an effort to avoid "discrimination" or "alienation" of their Hispanic students by their non-Hispanic peers, and as a result the HSI designation may have a less obvious impact on institutional culture. Either way, HSIs are intentional in creating programs and services that Hispanic cultures are celebrated and empowered which may be visible across your campus.

## College and University Mission and Value Statements

Colleges and universities have a mission statement, and oftentimes a vision statement, set of core values, strategic goals, objectives, outcomes, and/or creed in addition to the mission statement. Mission statements serve as symbolic representations of colleges and universities and contribute to strategic planning, represent how they see themselves, and often include a commitment to improving economic and/or social conditions of the region or state they serve. With the help of vision and other statements, mission statements can provide a blueprint of what students can expect from their college or university. Examples include commitments to inclusion and diversity, research, service to the community, excellence in teaching, or religious affiliation. Students new to a college or university should be familiar with mission statements, etc. and should find ways of taking advantage of resources as well as contributing to them as they can. Below is an example mission statement from The University of Alabama.

> *"The University of Alabama will advance the intellectual and social condition of the people of the state, the nation and the world through the creation, translation and dissemination of knowledge with an emphasis on quality programs in the areas of teaching, research, and service."*

## College Traditions

Your college or university likely has unique traditions that members of the university and/or local community participate in. It is important for students to participate in traditions at their institution so that they can experience aspects of what make their institution unique. Traditions are oftentimes originally developed by students and are a lot of fun! Other traditions may be the honoring of student academic or other achievements, or pep rally-like events prior to athletics contests. Example traditions include architecture students building a giant dragon that does battle with a giant phoenix built by engineering students at Cornell University, a 46-hour dance marathon at Penn State University that raises money for charity, a snowball fight between cadets and civilians at Virginia Tech during the first big snowfall of the year, and a go-kart race held each spring at Purdue University.

## Athletics

College athletics is another excellent example of an aspect of institutional culture that are vastly different depending on your college or university. Some colleges and universities utilize their athletics brand as a tool for recruitment, and could possibly be a reason why you attend the institution that you do. Athletics at these institutions are often a major part of the culture while at other colleges and universities there are small or no athletics department at all. Colleges and universities belonging to large athletic conferences like the Southeastern Conference and Big Ten Conference are more likely to offer many different men's and women's sports as well as many opportunities for student fans to get involved in athletics beyond the competitions themselves. Intercollegiate athletics not only provide opportunities for competition for athletes, but can also provide fun and exciting opportunities for nonathletes to become engaged with their institution's culture.

---

### DISCOVERY

1. What are some major aspects of my college or university's culture?

   _____

   _____

   _____

2. Are there historical contributions to your college or university's culture that I can identify?

   _____

   _____

   _____

3. What are the traditions on my campus that I would like to experience?

   _____

   _____

   _____

---

# Faculty at Your College or University

The word "faculty" derives from the Latin term *facultas*, which means *power* or *capability*. In short, college faculty are people who have the knowledge, skills and ability to teach you the subject matter covered in the classes you are taking. The faculty for your classes may represent a variety of roles at your college or university. They might be assistant, associate, or full professors (professional ranks achieved by meeting research, service and teaching benchmarks), graduate students (enrolled in masters or doctoral-level study, often with an assistantship or financial award that requires them to teach), instructors (full-time or part-time positions dedicated exclusively to teaching) or adjunct instructors (full-time administrative staff with a one-course teaching appointment, or experts hired to teach just one or two classes). Faculty teach different kinds of classes such as lectures, labs, seminars, or recitations. Regardless of their particular role within your college, your faculty will have knowledge and experience specific to the subject(s) they teach, and will set the tone for the style, delivery and expectations of the classes you are taking.

While it may be tempting at times to see your faculty as an antagonist or an enemy who might test you unexpectedly or give you large reading assignments, they *really are* on your side. They want to see you successfully learn the subject matter so that you can master it and build the foundation to your future college degree and career goals. So, when faculty invite you to a review session, or to office hours (a fancy way of saying *student* hours – the hours your faculty person is available to meet with you, a student!), or even just to communicate by email or video-conference, take them up on the offer!

---

### DISCOVERY

1.  How many of my faculty have I personally met or corresponded with at this point in the term?

    _____

    _____

    _____

2.  What would the advantages be to connecting with my faculty for each class I am taking?

    _____

    _____

    _____

---

We have said before (in Chapter 1) that successful students attend every class meeting (they do not miss class except for illness or true emergency). Successful students also reach out to their faculty, attend office hours, ask questions after class, and send email about points they did not understand. If you choose to do these things, you will enjoy several benefits: 1) you will no longer be anonymous – you will know your faculty and your faculty will know you; 2) you will actually understand your class material better because you will have talked in more depth with your faculty person about it after or outside of class; 3) you may even grow your network, forging close connections with some faculty who could later serve as mentors or references during your degree and career preparation process.

In Chapter 1, you examined the syllabus for each course to find out what was expected, how your grade would be determined, when your tests and major projects would be due, and to develop a study plan. Now, it's time to go back to the syllabus to find out how best to communicate and meet with your faculty. Use the end-of-chapter activity titled "Syllabus exploration: faculty communication" to make notes about office hours and preferred method of contact. Make a point of getting to know your faculty by attending office hours or speaking with them after class and get comfortable with sending email as well.

## Communicating with Faculty and University Staff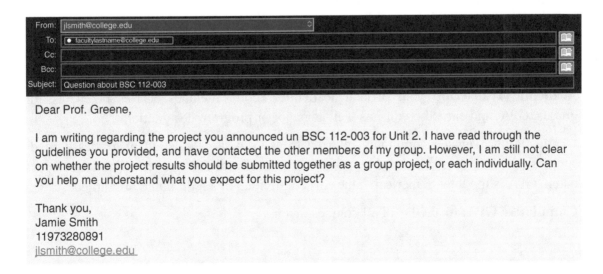

Note that some faculty outline in their syllabus exactly how they want you to communicate with them, and what identifying information you should include in an email to them (such as your full name, class and section, and/or student ID or student email). Here are some general guidelines for any email to college faculty or staff:

1. Write a subject line that clearly identifies the purpose of your email. For instance, "Subject: Question" is not specific enough. Instead, use a subject that directly mentions the class or topic in question, such as "Subject: Question about BSC 112-003," or "Subject: Question about First-Year Advising"

2. Begin your email with a respectful salutation, using the title or honorific appropriate to their role at your college (unless they have specifically requested that you address them in some other way). You might begin your email with "Dear Prof. Smith," or "Hello Dr. Greene."

3. In the body of the email, communicate as clearly as possible. State your question or communication in clear, complete, direct language, using correct grammar, spelling and punctuation. A message like, "I have a question about my test" is not specific enough. Instead, give details that will allow your email recipient to understand your question completely. For instance, "I am a student in Biology 112-003 and I have a question about whether Test 2 covers lecture topics only, or lecture and lab combined" asks a specific question about a specific test, and provides necessary information about which class section the writer is referencing.

4. Close the email using a closing salutation (such as Thank you, or Sincerely) followed on the next line by your signature block. Your signature block should include your full name and other identifying information such as your student ID and/or email.

Taking these simple steps will make it easiest for your faculty person (who may be teaching many students) to understand exactly who you are and what your question or communication is, so that they can respond to you directly.

Image example:

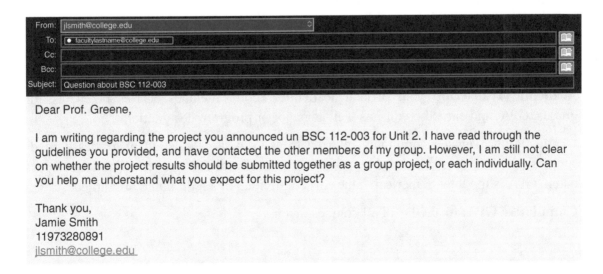

Consider your email with faculty as professional communication, and an opportunity for you to practice communication skills you will continue to use throughout college and into your future career.

> "I have personally struggled with a course and have found that setting up a meeting with the professor over Zoom or in person can show the professor that you care about your grades and excelling in the course. During this meeting, you can explain what have been doing to study and where you are having trouble. Meetings can also make the process of getting to know your professor more personal. As a new freshman, it is definitely worth your while to get to know your professors, so that you can be set up to be as successful as possible your first year."
>
> — Jordan S., senior, Public Health

## College Vocabulary

If you have ever traveled into a new environment with a different culture than what you are accustomed to, you know there is often a language or dialect to learn. Coming to a new college or university is no different. You should become familiar with important terms that you are likely to come across as a student. Below are lists of terms, phrases, and personnel that are helpful to know.

**Catalog:** a collection of academic policies, procedures, curriculums, and course descriptions within the college or university. You are assigned a catalog year when you begin a program, for which they must follow guidelines to achieve their degree or certificate.

**Withdrawal:** can refer to you removing yourself from a course (also known as drop), a semester or term, or the university entirely.

**Elective:** a course that is not a requirement for graduation based on a chosen curriculum, but often counts as credits toward graduation.

**Curriculum:** the collection of required classes for a major, minor, program, etc. Can also refer to what will be covered in a specific course.

**Credits or Credit Hours:** numbers assigned to courses designating their worth in progress toward graduation, usually assigned based on the number of required meeting hours per week. A typical major at a 4-year college or university requires at least 120 credits.

**Academic Transcript:** your official academic record. Includes classes taken, assigned grades, GPA, and earned credits, as well as major or program designation.

**Grade Point Average:** commonly referred to as GPA, a calculation of grades earned in courses taken. GPA is calculated by assigning a numerical value to letter grades of courses taken. GPA is the total numerical value earned, divided by credit hours attempted.

**Cumulative GPA:** total GPA of all courses taken.

**Semester or Term GPA:** GPA for a given semester or term.

**College or University GPA:** GPA for courses taken at a given college or university.

**Full-Time Enrollment:** when a student enrolls in at least the minimum number of credit hours for full-time student status, generally 12 credits for a regular fall or spring terms. These numbers are pretty standard, but can be different depending on term duration (such as quarter-term systems).

**Part-Time Enrollment:** when a student enrolls in less credits than the full-time enrollment minimum. Part-time enrollment can have an effect on financial aid and scholarships, on-campus residency, and others.

**Registration:** period when students can enroll in courses.

**University Registrar:** office who manages the university catalog, transcripts, credit inquiries such as transfer, the academic calendar, and others.

**Syllabus:** an outline or guide for a course. Syllabi usually include learning outcomes, procedures, expectations, grading structure, assignments, and a course schedule. Syllabi are provided to students when courses begin and serve as a "contract" between instructor and students.

**Major:** your primary field of study and what you venture to achieve a degree in. Majors include specific courses and credit hour requirements.

**Minor:** a secondary field of study, with fewer required credit hours than a major. Oftentimes majors also require a minor.

**Specialization or Concentration:** a specialization most commonly within a major. Does not exist in all majors.

**General Education:** sometimes known as liberal studies or core curriculum, predetermined categories of classes designed to give all undergraduates a well-rounded education outside of their program of study. General education categories often include English, writing, math, sciences, humanities, and others where students choose classes from a predetermined pool. General education is generally 40-50 credits total.

**Office Hours:** times during the week set aside by faculty to meet with you individually.

**Academic Advisor:** sometimes called just an advisor, your advisor helps you navigate the general education and your major curriculum by helping you identify classes and when to enroll in them. Depending on your college's advising structure, an advisor may also provide academic coaching or other services to help you navigate your college environment.

**Counselor:** counselors are experts for a given topic, most often mental health or career navigation.

1.  Are there other college terms you have heard and are unsure what they mean? If so, write them down and discover the definition.

_____

_____

_____

## Activating Your Brain for Learning

We have encountered many students who found that their first year of college was considerably more difficult than their high school courses had been, and a few who found the opposite to be true. Regardless of your previous learning experiences, though, you are bound to encounter classes in college that challenge you, whether in your first year or later on. If you are in classes that challenge you right now, this textbook is designed to help you with learning strategies that will see you through to degree completion.

Current brain science reveals that there are several different elements that make learning easier for humans. Our brains have developed to seek rewards, to be curious about novelty or things that are new to us, and to be attracted to social situations. In an educational setting, this means that we learn best when we perceive that there is a reward for learning, when we are interested in or curious about the new information presented, and when we are situated within a social context. You can take intentional steps to connect to all three of these and increase your own brain's receptivity to learning!

1.  **Reward:** some students are intrinsically motivated by long-term rewards. For example, Brittany might say to herself "I plan to be a doctor, and getting into a good medical school will be my reward for doing well in my classes and achieving my pre-med Biology degree." Some students are more motivated by short-term rewards. Paul might say to himself "I really need a reward at the end of each week in order to focus on studying for five days in a row." The good news is, you can and should build your own short-term rewards into your schedule! Paul could create his own short-term reward like so: "I need to study in order to do well in this class, so I have made a plan to study 5 hours this week. Once I complete my 5 hours, I will reward myself by going out with my friends."

2.  **Curiosity/novelty:** Throughout college, you will probably find that some classes are very interesting to you on their own, because you enjoy the professor's style or are curious about the subject matter. Other classes might feel less naturally interesting to you, but you don't want to let lack of interest prevent you from learning and achieving your goals. For those classes, you can adopt an inquiry-based learning method to "wake up" your brain's focus and curiosity, by asking questions and talking through material as you learn it. You will get to try this method below.

3.  **Social learning:** Learning becomes social when you are learning with others! Find a study buddy or a study group for each of your classes. Try out tutoring, coaching or mentoring as these provide additional ways to engage socially around your learning.

Attending faculty office hours is a way of making your learning more social. While class-related social connections are different from purely social events, taking opportunities to connect with others around learning will help you see new perspectives, learn new and effective ways to study, give you the chance to talk through questions and problems (activating your brain's curiosity), and build your support network throughout your college experience.

"When I set goals for myself, I usually set them by a daily basis. Like, finish problem 1 on Homework 3, or study for this midterm at least 30 minutes today, etc. One tip I use to stay motivated for my goals is to write little motivational sayings in my planner, like "halfway through the semester", or "almost done", etc. I also list out what goals I have for certain days in my planner so I can cross them out when I get done. When I complete a goal, I usually reward myself by having a little snack or watching an episode of a show on Netflix."

— Cody H., senior, Aerospace Engineering

## Inquiry-Based Study: Asking Questions and Talking it Out

Even when some of your lecture classes may consist of the faculty person presenting knowledge and information to you, which you then learn and internalize, you can use an inquiry-based study method (asking questions and talking it out) to help yourself learn the material. As you read your textbook and study your notes, make a habit of asking "why?" or "how?" or "what is this about?" or "what does this mean?" of each concept you encounter. As you study, make note of whether you can answer your own "why?", "how?", and "what?" questions.

**Try it:** Imagine you are enrolled in a Biology class, and that the following reading about metabolic pathways contains information that you need to understand to pass an upcoming test. Start by reading this passage from *Concepts of Biology*, made available through openstax.org.

### Metabolic Pathways

Consider the metabolism of sugar. This is a classic example of one of the many cellular processes that use and produce energy. Living things consume sugars as a major energy source, because sugar molecules have a great deal of energy stored within their bonds. For the most part, photosynthesizing organisms like plants produce these sugars. During photosynthesis, plants use energy (originally from sunlight) to convert carbon dioxide gas ($CO_2$) into sugar molecules (like glucose: $C_6H_{12}O_6$). They consume carbon dioxide and produce oxygen as a waste product. This reaction is summarized as:

$$6CO_2 + 6H_2O \rightarrow C_6H_{12}O_6 + 6O_2$$

1. Based on what you just read, how much could you explain out loud to a friend or classmate right now, without looking back at the reading?

2. If you were already familiar with this subject matter, you might be able to explain what you just read fairly well, thanks to your prior learning of similar material. However, if

you were previously unfamiliar with this subject, you may have found it difficult to tell your classmate or friend much at all about what you just read. How many times would you need to read it, to learn it well enough to explain it to someone else? 3 times? 5 times? More?

3.  This is a case in which inquiry-based reading practices (asking questions, talking it out) can help you process and remember what you are reading.

4.  Try it with questions: read the passage again, slowly enough to ask questions and talk through the causes and effects as you go. The following example serves as a guide:

*What is this about?*   *It's about*

### Metabolic Pathways

Consider the metabolism of sugar. This is a classic example of one of the many cellular processes that use and *How do they produce energy?* *Why?* produce energy. Living things consume sugars as a major energy source, because sugar molecules have a great deal of energy stored within their bonds. For the most part, photosynthesizing organisms like plants *How?* produce these sugars. During photosynthesis, plants use energy (originally from sunlight) to convert carbon *What is the result?* dioxide gas ($CO_2$) into sugar molecules (like glucose: $C_6H_{12}O_6$). They consume carbon dioxide and produce oxygen as a waste product. This reaction is summarized as:

$$6CO_2 + 6H_2O \rightarrow C_6H_{12}O_6 + 6O_2$$

5.  Now that you have worked through this passage asking questions about cause and effect, could you explain what you read to a friend or a classmate? How about the chemical reaction at the end of the paragraph? This provides a good opportunity to "talk it out". Instead of viewing the chemical reaction as a confusing jumble of letters and numbers, break it down piece by piece, talking it out as you go:

*What does this mean?*

*Talk it out:*   $6CO_2 + 6H_2O \rightarrow C_6H_{12}O_6 + 6O_2$

*6 carbon dioxide molecules plus 6 water molecules yield 1 glucose molecule plus 6 oxygen molecules.*

Building inquiry-based learning practices (asking questions, talking it out) is something you can do on your own, but it can be even more effective in a group setting! Brain science tells us that igniting curiosity by asking questions, and finding ways to make learning social, are *both* excellent ways to activate the brain for learning. For classes that are especially difficult for you, we recommend finding ways to connect with others over class material, creating opportunities to ask questions and talk the material out in the company of others. These opportunities could include:

• Joining or create a study group with others in your class

• Attending tutoring for that subject at your college's academic support center

• Going to a helpdesk or office hours offered by a graduate assistant for your class

• Attending office hours with the faculty person(s) for your class

**DISCOVERY**

1. Which of my classes are the most difficult so far?

   _____

   _____

   _____

2. Which of my class readings/texts are the most difficult to read and remember?

   _____

   _____

   _____

3. What rewards can I establish that will motivate me to study and learn?

   _____

   _____

   _____

4. Where could I apply an inquiry-based practice to learn and understand the material better?

   _____

   _____

   _____

5. For what classes would I benefit from a study group, tutoring, or other social learning opportunity?

   _____

   _____

   _____

6. What steps am I going to take in that direction?

   _____

   _____

   _____

## Overcoming Stress for Better Learning

Brain science also reveals that negative emotions and fear make it much harder for humans to learn. Your brain is a complex organ, and this discussion will focus on three main areas:

- The brain stem, which controls autonomic functions like breathing and heartbeat, and which is also the seat of our survival instincts. When we are in danger, our brain stem directs a variety of survival behaviors such as fight, flight, or freeze. We will explore these in greater depth below.

- The limbic system, which processes emotional information and our emotional responses.
- The neocortex, the outer layer of the human brain which is used for reasoning, problem-solving, and self-awareness.

## Figure 2.3:   Three Areas of the Human Brain.

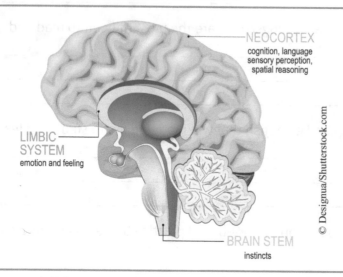

Here is an example of how stress affects learning: If you feel anxious about learning math, for instance, and if you have had negative experiences learning math in the past, the activation of your brain's emotional centers (limbic system) around these negative feelings, paired with your brain stem's survival response to stress (fight-flight-freeze), actually pulls blood flow and neuronal activity away from your brain's cerebral cortex, which is needed for reasoning and problem-solving. It's difficult to learn math (or science, or any subject) when your brain's center for conscious thinking and learning is impaired or inaccessible.

**It works like this:**

Negative feelings about the past or your present experience activate the limbic system, bringing up feelings of stress and anxiety.

Stress and anxiety feel like danger, and ignite the brain stem's survival instincts. These survival instincts helped long-ago humans survive the dangers of life, protecting them from predators and natural disasters. For instance, if you were trying to avoid being eaten by a tiger you might **fight** the tiger in hopes of impairing it or making it leave you alone, you might take **flight** by running from the tiger, or you might **freeze** by hiding or simply holding very still in hopes the tiger won't see you. The same survival instincts kick in for current-day humans under any kind of stress, and they can work against you if you are stressed while trying to learn.

Imagine that you are studying for a math test and you start to become very stressed as you struggle with difficult material. Under stress, your survival instincts kick in and your brain tells you to fight, take flight, or freeze. In this situation, those instincts don't really help you. Fighting math and hoping it will leave you alone patently doesn't work (it wasn't trying to eat you, and the test is still next week). Running away from math (flight) by avoiding your studies for days or weeks on end also doesn't help as it ultimately places you further behind in your learning. Taking the freeze approach (holding very still, hoping math will go away) stops your progress and puts you even further behind. Worst of all, when you are in survival mode your cerebral cortex can become so inactive (in favor of all the activity happening in the brain stem and limbic system) that your mind can literally go blank on everything you were just trying to learn.

The good news is, there are steps you can take to calm your survival instincts and your limbic system, and return your cerebral cortex to its learning-capable purpose. If you find that you are becoming anxious while learning – you are thinking negative or "I can't" thoughts, your heart is racing, or you just can't focus on the material in front of you – try one of these calming methods to bring your brain back into balance:

1. Replace "I can't" with "I can." Actively tell yourself "I can do this. I can figure this out." If you consciously decide to stop reinforcing or repeating a negative thought, it will often dissipate quickly, though it may then try to reassert itself. Because it can be hard to "just stop" if your negative thought is looping (repeating), consciously replacing it with a positive thought is often the easiest way to break that negative cycle.

2. Take five (or more) deep breaths. Breathing in through your nose to a slow count of four, and out through your mouth to another slow count of four, actually signals to your brain that all is well, and that it can return to a state of calm. After five breaths, you will probably find that your heart rate is slowing and you can focus again.

3. Get active and go outside. Regular exercise has been shown to reduce stress and anxiety in general. In addition, getting outside can help in a moment of particular stress or anxiety. Research has shown that moving from an enclosed space to an open, expansive, outdoor space, increases the neuropeptide oxytocin which in turn increases your sense of confidence and safety. As you feel better, you are better able to focus on your studies.

---

**DISCOVERY**

1. Are there subjects I feel very anxious about learning, or feel I cannot learn? How do I feel when I try to study for these subjects? What works best for me to regain a sense of calm and focus?

_____

_____

_____

---

## Setting SMART Goals

Have you ever set goals that you easily achieved? Have you ever set goals that you failed to achieve? Thinking back, was there a particular difference in those goals or in how you set them? Many things can influence how committed we are to our goals. Having accountability (other people who are helping us stay committed to our goals), or having a personal passion or drive to achieve particular goals, can both increase the chance that we achieve them. Another way to ensure we meet our goals is to make them SMART. SMART is an acronym that helps us remember that goals should be

- Specific
- Measurable
- Achievable
- Relevant
- Time-bound

For example, you might set a goal to "study a lot" for your chemistry class, because you want to earn a passing grade on the first test. However, that goal is not very well defined and it's not really clear exactly what achieving that goal would look like. Let's see if we can refine this goal and make it SMART.

**S** - To make the goal **specific**, you could refine it to "study chemistry notes after lecture." (This goal pertaining to studying notes would be *in addition to* reading the textbook, which might be covered by another SMART goal or study plan).

**M** - To make it **measurable**, decide on a length of time, or a number of pages, that you wish to study. For this example, let's say "study chemistry notes for 45 minutes after every lecture."

**A** - This goal is also **achievable** – meaning that it is something you can realistically accomplish. In this case, 45 minutes seems like a manageable amount of time to study your notes (in addition to the time you are spending reading the textbook before lectures).

**R** - The goal is **relevant** because it relates directly to what you are trying to achieve – understand and learn your chemistry notes in order to be prepared for the upcoming test.

**T** - Finally, you can make this goal **time-bound** by putting an overall time limit on it. For instance, your goal could be "I will study my chemistry notes for 45 minutes after every lecture until the first test." After that first chemistry test, you can re-evaluate this goal and decide whether to continue with a similar goal, or whether you should increase or decrease the time you spend studying your notes, or focus on other subjects.

SMART goals help you make the best use of the time you have, help you focus your study so that your precious time is not wasted, and can help you work toward a life balance that allows time for study, commitments, social life, and self-care.

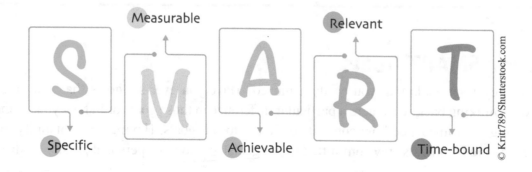

© Kritt789/Shutterstock.com

1. Based on what I have learned about SMART goals, how many of my current goals are already "SMART"? How could I reframe them to make them "SMART"?

_____

_____

_____

# Self-care: Taking Good Care of Yourself

College can be an exciting time, but it is also demanding. You are facing several challenges like school, social life, family, work and other obligations. You may be handling more of these challenges on your own than you ever have in the past, and you are working hard to keep them in balance. It is very important, especially now, that you take good care of yourself and your health – physical, mental and emotional.

*Now* is the right time to establish health and wellness practices that will carry you through graduation and beyond. In order to thrive, you need to have proper nutrition, physical fitness, stress relief, and good sleep habits. Setting habits now for physical, mental and emotional health will offer you a lifetime of benefits.

Nutrition: The average college freshman gains 5 pounds, and many students gain more over four years. Habits like eating on the go, not looking at serving sizes and ingredients, eating out rather than cooking in, and stress snacking, can all contribute to unwanted weight gain.

Here are some tips for eating and staying healthy:

- Avoid liquid calories. Drinking water instead of sodas, lattes, sweetened teas, fruit juices, and alcohol, can significantly lower your caloric intake.

- Watch your portions, especially when eating out. A study reported in Science Daily found 92% of large-chain and nonchain restaurants served meals that exceeded recommended calorie requirements for a single meal. Cooking at home will save on cash and calories. When you do eat out, plan ahead to share a dish with a friend, or eat half and take the other half home for a meal the next day.

- Focus on fruits and vegetables. The USDA recommends eating five servings per day of fruits and vegetables in order to get adequate vitamins and fiber, maintain a healthy weight, and protect against diseases in the long term. An easy way to do this is to fill half your plate with fruits and veggies at every meal and every snack. Eating adequate fruits and veggies per day is a health habit you can set now that will benefit you for the rest of your life!

Physical Fitness: Being too inactive or sedentary is linked to long-term health problems like heart disease, diabetes, and high blood pressure. In addition, there are positive correlations between regular exercise, memory function and learning in young adults. According to the Centers for Disease Control, you should aim for at least 2.5 hours of moderate-intensity exercise each week, and participate in muscle-strengthening exercise at least twice per week. Here are some ways to incorporate exercise into your weekly routine:

- Commute by walking or biking to class or to work.

- Make study breaks exercise breaks by taking a quick walk or doing some quick exercises like lifting free weights or climbing a few flights of stairs.

- Find a fun way to workout at college. Join an intramural sports team, take a dance or yoga class, or meet up with friends at the gym for basketball.

**Stress Management:**  Chronic stress can lead to many negative health effects, including illness, headaches, insomnia and decreased productivity. Long-term stress can lead to obesity, heart disease, high blood pressure and diabetes. It's normal to be stressed some of the time, but living with stress constantly can really hurt you. The use of alcohol and mind-altering substances may alleviate stress, but they are maladaptive because they can compromise your health and safety. Here are some positive ways to combat stress:

- Pay attention to warning signs. Often your body gives you the first signals that you are stressed, with warning signs such as headache, upset stomach, rapid heartbeat, loss of appetite or intense cravings, or irritability.

- Practice stress-relieving techniques. Trying to power through tasks or study while stressed actually makes you less productive. It's better to deal with your stress when it is happening. Taking even a 5-minute break to alleviate stress can help you in the long run. Try taking a brisk walk, doing deep breathing exercises or meditation, talking with a friend, or doing an activity you enjoy. Any of these actions gives your brain a break from whatever is stressing you so that you can return to what you were doing in a more relaxed state.

- Make happiness a priority. Actively choose to do things that make you happy on a daily basis. Cultivating happiness lowers your cortisol (a stress hormone) and helps you reduce feelings of stress and anxiety.

- Talk it out. Expressing feelings of stress is an effective way to release them. Talk with friends, family, or a professional therapist about how you are feeling.

**Sleep and Rest:**  Adults need adequate rest for their minds and bodies to function best. The National Heart, Lung and Blood Institute states that adults need at least 7 to 8 hours per night of continuous sleep. A good pillow, proper nutrition and regular exercise will all help improve sleep. Here are further tips on getting a good night's sleep:

- Relax before bedtime. About an hour before bedtime, shut off all electronic devices, make your to-do list for tomorrow (so you know your plan and won't be kept up worrying), take deep breaths, do gentle yoga poses or stretches, and take a shower or a bath.

- Cool down your room. The temperature of your room can affect sleep. Most people sleep better in a room that is slightly cool, between 60 and 67 degrees. If your roommates don't like it that cool, consider investing in a fan to keep your space cooler.

- Make your bed a sleep-only zone. When you work in bed, you will associate that area with work instead of sleep. Also, looking at a screen reduces melatonin, a hormone that helps you fall asleep and stay asleep. Set habits that help you associate your bed with sleeping and resting, and not with working or worrying.

---

**DISCOVERY**

1. Of the wellness areas above (nutrition, physical fitness, stress management, and sleep/rest), which is currently going well for me? Which could use some more attention? What are two positive steps I could take toward better wellness?

   _____

   _____

   _____

---

"As a first-year student I struggled with delegating tasks and taking personal time for myself to decompress. I feel that not taking time to relax or take your mind off of school can cause burnout a lot sooner than one would think. Burnout can lead to lack of motivation and stress, which is no help to a successful college student. I would strongly advise taking a walk with friends around campus, sitting on the quad, or even going to the gym to give yourself a mental break. I swear by these methods and they still help me to this day."

— Jordan S., senior, Public Health

"During my freshman year I struggled with giving myself time to relax and enjoy free time. I would do a lot of school work with little to no breaks at all. My advice to first year students is to take breaks and make sure to get enough sleep. When you try to pull an all-nighter or cram the night before an exam and only get a couple hours of sleep, your brain doesn't function as well as if you had gotten 7-8 hours of sleep. Another tip is to take a break in between completing assignments, don't feel like you have to do all your work for every class in one sitting, it never hurts to take a short 20–30-minute break and relax."

— Cody H., senior, Aerospace Engineering

## Homesickness

Homesickness is a common challenge for new college students, especially for those who are attending a college or university a long way from home, or those who do not have friends or siblings also attending the same college or university. Homesickness does not discriminate by college or university size, type, or location and is something that new college students should anticipate and prepare for. Below is a list of strategies that students can utilize to combat homesickness.

- **Engage with the campus community and get out of your room:** Whether joining university sponsored organizations or clubs, getting involved in academic, social, or athletic events, attending residence hall meetings, or just getting out and talking with residence hall neighbors, students should get out of their rooms and talk with people. While binging Netflix or Hulu or playing video games are good ways of relaxing, engaging with others are important to your mental health as well.

- **Make your place of residence feel like home:** This might mean photos of family and friends, trinkets from home, or just decorating in a way that is comfortable for you.

- **Make a plan for calling home:** Making a plan for calling or video chatting with family or friends can help combat homesickness. Calling home too often, however, can increase homesickness because not enough attention can be paid for engaging with the campus community.

- **Stay busy:** Whether you choose to focus on coursework, clubs, or social activities, stay busy. Keeping your mind active can be a distraction from missing family and friends.

- **Limit social media exposure:** Of course you should stay connected with friends and family on your social media of choice, but not checking it all of the time is positive as well. Implementing a strategy of only checking social media is a good study strategy too!

- **Explore your new surroundings, including what is off-campus:** A way of engaging with any new environment is seeing what it has to offer. Sometimes new students limit their exposure to campus only, don't forget that the community you are in likely has restaurants, shopping, or recreation that you may find enjoyable!

- **Give yourself time:** As is the case in any environment, feeling uncomfortable early is common. Try not to decide in your first semester that your college or university isn't for you and subsequently make a plan for leaving. Instead, make a plan for staying that should include getting more connected to your university and the people there.

- **Don't compare yourself to others:** While homesickness can affect all students, it doesn't, and oftentimes students who are experiencing it are also good at hiding it. Social media is notorious for just showing what is going well in people's lives, so don't compare your happiness with theirs.

- **Do something for yourself each day:** Really just a way of improving mental health and happiness, doing something for you each day can be a way of combating homesickness as well.

- **Ask for help:** Students experiencing extreme or consistent levels of homesickness that are keeping you from attending class, completing homework, or engaging with peers should see what resources are available through their campus counseling or mental health support office. These offices frequently help students experiencing homesickness with a variety of resources.

- **Exercise:** Physical health is correlated to mental health and can be a wonderful stress relief option. Students who like to exercise with others but do not yet have a workout buddy can visit the campus recreation office for options that may include many different exercise class options, intramural sports, or even trips off campus to local community recreation options.

"One of my biggest adjustments coming into college was making sure I was eating enough good stuff. As weird at it might sound, it is easy to forget to eat or even just try and sustain yourself on chips which ultimately is unhealthy and can sometimes hinder your overall performance in other areas. Many people coming to college are used to being able to just walk to their pantry and get food. Also, many individuals never had to think about if they had a balanced diet because meals were prepared for them. Therefore, it is a learning curve that I personally had to be conscious of when deciding to fill my nutritional needs."

— Mae F., freshman, Management

## Common Barriers to College Success according to Research

Colleges and universities are interested in doing what they can to make sure students remain consistently enrolled in classes and graduate. As a way of supporting students during their college experience, colleges and universities pay attention to student risk factors, or factors that may contribute to students not remaining enrolled in classes. While a single risk factor may be the sole reason students do not enroll or stop attending, often students' decision to not continue classes are a result of multiple contributing factors. The purpose of this section is to help you find ways of combating them. The chart below describes some of the most common risk factors that can lead to students' not remaining enrolled in college.

| Risk Factor | Solution |
| --- | --- |
| **Cost of attendance** refers to the total cost of going to college including tuition, fees, housing, dining, textbook costs, and other ancillary costs which may include commuting to campus and materials. | Visit your campus financial aid and scholarships offices, as well as seek out financial assistance opportunities offered by your major. There are also many private scholarship opportunities that can be found on the internet with a quick search. Students should consider lower cost options of housing and dining if they can to cut unnecessary costs. Many students also take on part-time jobs, though working more than 10-20 hours per week can have a negative effect on student success. |
| **Academic consistency** is often measured by GPA, and high school GPA is a common predictor of college student success. On average, the higher high school GPA a student has, the more likely they are to remain enrolled and graduate. | Fortunately, high school GPA doesn't follow you to college, everyone has a clean GPA slate when they first arrive. Consistent academic success begins with class attendance, turning assignments in, and actively participating in classes and discussions. Successful students also utilize campus academic support resources such as coaching, tutoring, and skill development sessions. Old habits can die hard, but making a commitment to consistent academic engagement can greatly improve grades and GPA. |

*(Continued...)*

| Risk Factor | Solution |
| --- | --- |
| **Sex, race, and gender**: Asian and White college students consistently remain continuously enrolled and graduate at higher rates than do other races, as do women compared to men. While sex, race, and gender themselves are not risk factors, characteristics attributed to each can be, such as the experiencing of discrimination. | While it is unlikely for students to avoid experiencing discrimination entirely, students may be able to find solace or support from multicultural or gender service centers or student-led organizations on their campus. |
| **Generational status** refers to whether or not students have immediate family members who have completed a 4-year degree. Students who have immediate family members who have completed a degree consistently persist and graduate at higher levels than students considered to the first-generation, or students without immediate family members who have completed a 4-year degree. | Differences in college success between first-generation (FGS) and other students tend to be attributed to demographic and familial characteristics, as well as financial and educational disadvantages FGS students are more likely to encounter. Because FGS students often do not have a family member familiar with college procedure and challenges students encounter, FGS students should consult resources such as their academic advisor or faculty when they need help navigating the college environment. |
| **Social capital** are resources inherent in social relations that facilitate collective action and include trust, norms, and networks of association representing a group that congregates regularly for a common purpose. Students who do not develop relationships with faculty, staff, peers, and family members lack social capital, making it difficult to navigate the college environment and feel supported. | Students should work to develop a network of support consisting of faculty, staff, peers, and family. Networks of relationships can assist students in managing an otherwise unfamiliar environment by providing students with valuable information, guidance, and emotional support. |
| **Satisfaction** in the college experience serves as a contributing factor to student college success, but also the result of other factors. Students satisfied with their college experience are more likely to remain enrolled and graduate from that college or university. | The college experience has a reputation of helping students discover themselves and find what interests and drives them. It can also be a great place to meet new people and have a lot of fun! Students should get outside of their comfort zone when it comes to new experiences and follow their academic, social, and involvement desires to find their own individual level of satisfaction. |
| **Belonging**: From a higher education perspective, belonging refers to "students' perceived social support on campus, a feeling or sensation of connectedness, the experience of mattering or feeling cared about, accepted, respected, valued by, and important to the group or others on campus (Strayhorn, 2012, p.3)." Like satisfaction, belonging can serve as a factor of college success. | Academic and social integration is closely associated to sense of belonging, and has long been identified as an important factor in college student success. |

**DISCOVERY**

1. Are you susceptible to any of the risk factors listed above? If so, do you think they have affected you in the past?

   _____

   _____

   _____

2. Choose a risk factor above and discuss how you can be proactive in making sure it does not affect you negatively.

   _____

   _____

   _____

3. List 1-2 other risk factors not listed above that you think affect college student success and why.

   _____

   _____

   _____

## Chapter Summary

Like an iceberg, only a fraction of you is visible on the surface. The 80% "below the surface", comprised of your character, self-discipline, values, hard work, and identity, support the 20% that is visible above the surface. It is important to make choices each day to achieve what you want to show to the world. Your college or university is also like an iceberg in that there is much under the surface that makes your college unique, including how and why it was established, its mission statement, its connection to a particular culture or religion, and its tradition. Part of your college experience includes discovering all of the wonderful and unique things your college has to offer.

At every college and university, successful college students are proactive in learning what the structure and culture offer them, and how they can take advantage of opportunities, while also avoiding pitfalls that they can control and preparing for those they can't. Students who make choices to learn actively, set goals, and stay healthy are much more likely to achieve college success during their first year than those who don't.

## End-of-Chapter Activities

I. **Attend Office Hours.** Attend office hours for each class, or stay and chat with each faculty person after class (if available) at least once. Before you go, prepare what you would like to say to your faculty person. This could be as simple as "I just wanted to introduce myself" or you might have a specific question about a concept from your reading or from class that you need help with.

II. **Write a Professional Email.** Write an email to one of your faculty, or to a staff member (like your advisor, or career center representative). If style or format are not described in the syllabus, here is a generic form you can use:

- Subject: Question about [class title and section, or other topic of communication]
- Salutation: Hello Prof. [Lastname] or Dear Dr. [Lastname]
- Body: State your question or communication clearly and directly, using correct grammar, spelling and punctuation.
- Closing salutation: Thank you, or Sincerely
- Signature: Your full name and any other identifying information (such as class number and section, and/or student ID)

III. **Practice De-Stressing.** During a study session, pay attention to whether you are becoming anxious or stressed. If you do begin to feel stressed, try one of the calming techniques described in the chapter. Decide which one, or combination, works best for you. (As a reminder, these techniques include replacing a negative thought with a positive one, taking 5 deep breaths, going outside for a few minutes, and doing something active for a few minutes)

IV. **Be a Social Learner.** Make learning social by joining a study group or finding a study partner for one or more classes.

V. **Create SMART Goals.** Create SMART goals related to study for two or more of your classes. Use the example in the chapter to develop your own goals that are Specific, Measurable, Achievable, Relevant, and Time-Bound.

VI. **Wellness Check**

## WELLNESS CHECK

Use the following wellness check-in to determine how you are doing in terms of self-care. Circle the statement that best represents your current practices

– I avoid sugary beverages such as sweetened coffee/tea, sodas, and juices          Always | Sometimes | Rarely | Never

– I limit my consumption of alcohol and mind-altering substances          Always | Sometimes | Rarely | Never

– I am mindful of caloric intake when eating out          Always | Sometimes | Rarely | Never

– I eat at least 5 fruits and vegetables per day OR I fill half my plate with fruits and veggies at every meal          Always | Sometimes | Rarely | Never

– I bike or walk to class or work          Always | Sometimes | Rarely | Never

– I do something physically active during quick study breaks          Always | Sometimes | Rarely | Never

– I workout or play a sport regularly          Always | Sometimes | Rarely | Never

– I notice when my body is showing signs that I am stressed or anxious          Always | Sometimes | Rarely | Never

– I take steps to alleviate stress when I am feeling stressed or anxious          Always | Sometimes | Rarely | Never

– I do deep breathing or meditation on a daily basis          Always | Sometimes | Rarely | Never

– I have friends and/or family I can talk to regularly, who help lower my feelings of stress or anxiety          Always | Sometimes | Rarely | Never

– I try to do something that makes me happy every day          Always | Sometimes | Rarely | Never

– I give myself an hour to relax and wind down before bed          Always | Sometimes | Rarely | Never

– I keep my bed as a sleep-only (not study and work) zone          Always | Sometimes | Rarely | Never

– I sleep 7-8 hours each night          Always | Sometimes | Rarely | Never

– I keep my room cool during sleep hours          Always | Sometimes | Rarely | Never

Which elements of your self-care are going really well?

_____

_____

Which ones are not going so well?

_____

_____

Choose one or two that you wish to improve on, and commit to those for the next three weeks. You could even create a SMART goal for them! At the end of three weeks, you will likely find that they have become easy and habitual for you.

# References

Adelman, C. (2006). *The toolbox revisited: Paths to degree completion from high school through college.* U.S. Department of Education, Office of Educational Research and Improvement.

Bess, J. L., & Dee, J. R., (2012). *Understanding college and university organization: Theories for effective policy and practice* (Vol 1). Stylus.

Bimper, A. Y. (2016). Capital matters: Social sustaining capital and the development of black student-athletes. *Journal of Intercollegiate Sport, 9*(1), 106–128.

Carter-Francique, A. R., Hart, A., & Cheeks, G. (2015). Examining the value of social capital and social support for black student-athletes' academic success. *Journal of African-American Studies, 19*(2), 157–177.

Center for Changing our Campus Culture. (2017). *A culturally specific perspective: The HBCU story.* http://changingourcampus.org/wp-content/uploads/2017/02/HBCU-Story-Final-2-21-17.pdf

Center for Community College Student Engagement (CCCSE). (2019). *Preserving culture and planning for the future: An exploration of student experiences at tribal colleges.* https://www.ccsse.org/center/SR2019/Tribal_Colleges.pdf

Choy, S. (2001). Students whose parents did not go to college: Postsecondary access, persistence, and attainment. National Center for Education Statistics. https://nces.ed.gov/pubs2001/2001126.pdf

Comoletti, J. (2014). The 20 best college traditions in the US. *Insider.* https://www.businessinsider.com/the-best-college-traditions-2014-7

Hoffman, M., Richmond, J., Morrow, J., & Salomone, K. (2002). Investigating sense of belonging in first year college students. *Journal of College Student Retention, 4*(3), 227–256.

Ishitani, T., & DesJardins, S. (2002). A longitudinal investigation of dropout from college in the United States. *Journal of College Students Retention: Research, Theory, and Practice, 4*(2), 173–201.

Kemper, D., & Leung, D. Y. P. (2004). Relationship between the employment of coping mechanisms and a sense of belonging for part-time students. *Educational Psychology, 24*(3), 345-357.

Kim, J. (2015). Predictors of college retention and performance between regular and special admissions. *Journal of Student Affairs Research and Practice, 52*(1), 50–63. https://doi: 10.1080/19496591.2015.995575

Motl, T. C., Multon, K. D., & Zhao, F. (2018). Persistence at a tribal university: factors associated with second year enrollment. *Journal of Diversity in Higher Education, 11*(1), 51–66. National Center for Education Statistics (NCES). (2020*). Fast facts: Historically Black colleges and universities.* https://nces.ed.gov/fastfacts/display.asp?id=667

National Center for Education Statistics. (2019). *Undergraduate retention and graduation rates.* https://nces.ed.gov/programs/coe/indicator_ctr.asp

National Research Council. (1995). Colleges of agriculture at the land grant universities: A profile. *The National Academies Press.* https://doi.org/10.17226/4980

New World Encyclopedia. (2008). *Normal school.* https://www.newworldencyclopedia.org/p/index.php?title=Normal_school&oldid=845599

Petty, T. (2014). Motivating first-generation students to academic success and college completion. *College Student Journal, 48*(1), 257–264.

Redford, J., & Hoyer, K. M. (2017). First-generation and continuing-generation college students: a comparison of high school and postsecondary experiences. *U.S. Department of Education.* https://files.eric.ed.gov/fulltext/ED575985.pdf

Shoulders, C. W., Edgar, L. D., & Johnson, D. M. (2019). The relationship between student admissions data and six-year degree completion. *Journal of Human Sciences and Extension, 7*(1), 104–116.

Thelin, J. R., Edwards, J. R., Moyen, E., Berger, J. B., & Calkins, M. V. (2021). Higher education in the United States: Historical development, system. *Education Encyclopedia-State University.com.* https://education.stateuniversity.com/pages/2044/Higher-Education-in-United-States.html

Tinto, V. (1975). Dropout from higher education: A theoretical synthesis of recent research. *Review of Educational Research, 45*(1), 89–125.

Tinto, V. (1993). *Leaving college: Rethinking the causes and cures of student attrition* (2nd ed.). University of Chicago Press.

Tinto, V. (1997). Colleges as communities: Exploring the educational character of student persistence. *Journal of Higher Education, 68*(6), 599–623.

U.S. Department of Education Office for Civil Rights. (1991). *Historically Black colleges and universities and higher education desegregation.* https://www2.ed.gov/about/offices/list/ocr/docs/hq9511.html

Velez, A. (2019). A critical interpretation of the Hispanic-serving institution designation effects on institutional identity. *Office of Community College Research and Leadership, 5*(2). https://files.eric.ed.gov/fulltext/ED595435.pdf

## Chapter 3

# Using Your Resources

| Choices of Successful Students | Choices of Struggling Students |
|---|---|
| 1. Connect with their advisor early. | 1. Wait until registration time to make an advising appointment. |
| 2. Know their college's general education and major/minor requirements and make a plan for which classes to enroll in future semesters. | 2. Rely on their academic advisor to tell them what classes to enroll in. |
| 3. Know where to find access to their transcript and track their own progress. | 3. Ignore their transcript and don't know requirements for graduation. |
| 4. Become financially literate and take control of their college finances. | 4. Do not create a spending plan for college and are at risk of higher amounts of debt or running out of money mid-semester. |
| 5. Utilize campus resources provided to them by their college or university. | 5. Try to solve challenges on their own without consulting campus resources. |
| 6. Plan ahead for exams and projects at midterm. | 6. Wait until the last minute to study or complete projects for midterms. |

## Introduction

This chapter is your opportunity to learn about the many resources your college offers, and how to access those resources. College resources and student services exist precisely because you are not intended to "go it alone." Your college wants you to have a positive and successful experience that culminates in you earning your degree, and they offer a wide array of student services and resources to help you accomplish just that.

**Focus Questions:**

1. What are some common resources colleges and universities offer, and how can they benefit you?
2. In what ways can you be a smart college consumer?

## Asking for What You Need

> "Asking for help isn't weak, it's a great example of how to take care of yourself"
>
> — Charlie Brown

Some college students have difficulty asking for help. Maybe they are worried they will look weak or will seem like they don't know what they are doing, maybe they are just shy, or maybe they are overwhelmed by the number of new things they have to deal with on a daily basis. If you relate to any of these, you are not alone! It is important to identify any inner obstacles that prevent you from asking for help, and then find ways to overcome them. As Charlie Brown says in the quote above, asking for help is part of good self-care. When you can identify your own questions or needs, and seek help for those, it's a way to demonstrate that you possess the self-confidence and the maturity to take good care of yourself.

**DISCOVERY**

1. When you need help or answers to something college-related, what do you do? Who do you ask? Do you find it difficult to ask for help?

_____

_____

_____

"I think a new freshman needs to know that they should not ever be embarrassed or scared to approach anyone for assistance. All college students and most employees on campus were in their same shoes at one point. I think new freshman need to also be made aware of the ample resources we have on campus to help them succeed as students."

— Payton M., senior, Psychology

"I would tell a freshman to be willing to ask questions, be willing to be vulnerable, and be willing to grow. These 4 years can really shape you so this is a great time to step out of your comfort zone and become who you want to become. Make sure to do your research and find out what your university has to offer. Also, when it comes to your knowledge and/or your well-being, you can never ask too many questions. So always ask until you feel content."

— Kenzie B., senior, Mechanical Engineering

# Academic Advising

Many college students think of an advisor as someone who tells them what classes to take. It is true that academic advisors make course recommendations for students, but depending on the advising structure of your college they may do much more! According to the National Academic Advising Association "through academic advising, students learn to become members of their higher education community, to think critically about their roles and responsibilities as students, and to prepare to be educated citizens of a democratic society and global community." In a nutshell, your academic advisor can help you navigate the college experience and develop life-long skill sets. In addition to helping you with course selection, advisors often serve as your coach for motivation and goal-setting, your guide for understanding academic requirements and for accessing campus-wide resources, and your advocate for academic success. Academic advisors are experts in navigating courses and credits, and are a great resource for questions related to general education, majors and minors, and other academic requirements.

## DISCOVERY

1. Who is my academic advisor? If I don't know who your advisor is, how can I find out?

   _____

   _____

   _____

2. How can I make an appointment with my academic advisor?

   _____

   _____

   _____

## General Education

You are likely enrolled in classes that belong to what universities call a general education, core curriculum, or liberal studies curriculum. The general education curriculum includes groups of courses that are designed to provide you a well-rounded college education, rather than taking only major or career-specific classes. Research indicates that overall, general education curricula help you improve your critical thinking skills, learn to communicate effectively, gain interpersonal skills, and acquire habits of mind that lead to lifelong learning. Your college may have a general education curriculum that also aims to help you develop additional skill sets such as engaging with the university community, becoming an empathetic and responsible citizen, or expanding your multicultural competence. In addition, the general education curriculum provides an opportunity for students who have not decided on a major to explore different disciplines.

The general education curriculum typically includes subject categories such as English and other languages, the arts, social sciences, humanities, and natural sciences. Many majors require their students take specific general education courses. Your academic advisor will help you identify those. For example, a macroeconomics course for business majors might also be considered a social science general education course. This overlap between the general education requirement and major requirements means that students can sometimes "double up" on graduation requirements, because a single class meets both requirements. Students who are undecided on their majors should think strategically and search for general education classes that are also required for majors they are considering. Academic advisors are a great resource to help you in this process. General education curricula are generally 40 to 50 credits and can take up much of your freshman and sophomore years (as junior standing or upper-class standing begins at 61 earned credit hours for many colleges). General education curricula are often similar to the courses and credits required for an associate's degree at a community college or other 2-year college. If you are considering taking summer classes, sometimes taking a general education course at your local community college is a good idea, but you should always check with your academic advisor first to make sure it will count toward your general education and/or your major at primary college or university.

## Discovery

1.  What are the categories for general education at my college or university, and how many credits must I complete to finish each category?

    _____

    _____

    _____

## Majors

By now you likely have chosen a major. Having a major is important because it not only gives you a specific course pathway for graduation, but it also gives you a deeper connection to others in your major and/or department. Once you have selected a major you will probably receive a great deal of communication from your academic advisor about opportunities such as study groups, professional organization opportunities, internship and career fair information, and other worthwhile information. It is important to engage with some of these opportunities so that you can actively grow your scholastic and professional network, and do not miss out on great opportunities! If you have not yet decided on a major, that's okay too. Many colleges and universities have academic advisors who specialize in exploratory (undecided) students or programs that help students select a major. If you need help deciding on a major, ask your academic advisor.

It goes without saying that your major classes prepare you for your career or graduate school. Freshman and sophomore level major classes are more likely to have many students in a single class and may include students with many different majors (e.g., students taking those classes for general education credit). Junior and senior level classes usually have fewer students per class and include students with the same or similar majors. Majors usually require that you not only pass major classes but that you meet specific academic requirements such as grade (e.g., must earn at least a "C") and GPA (e.g., must have at least a 3.0). If you don't know if your major carries these requirements or not, start by checking your major's website and if you cannot find the information you need, ask your academic advisor.

1.  What are the GPA and credit requirements for my major? If you are still exploring, choose your current top choice.

    _____

    _____

    _____

## Minors and Concentrations

While all students seeking a 4-year degree need a major (with the exception of nondegree seeking students), you may also be interested in or required to select a minor. Minors help you specialize or expand your skill sets and make you more competitive for future employment. Minors also add credits (typically 18–24) to your transcript. A typical minimum credit hour graduation requirement at a 4-year college or university is about 120 credits. Your minor may be helpful in reaching that minimum, especially if your major has a low number of required credits.

Concentrations (sometimes also known as specializations) provide a specialization or specific curriculum direction within a major. An example is a major in Apparel and Textiles with two concentration options – one in Design, and the other in Retail. A student with the Apparel and Textiles major and Design concentration is more likely interested in designing clothing, while the student in a Retail concentration is more likely interested in selling clothing for a career. Concentrations can be diverse in their number of credits. Like majors, minors and concentrations are likely to have course grade and overall GPA requirements. Not all majors have concentrations so don't worry if yours does not.

1.  Does my major require a minor or concentration? _____Yes _____No
2.  If so, what minor or concentration am I leaning toward?

    _____

    _____

    _____

## Course Delivery Options

During the COVID-19 that began in the year 2020 pandemic, course delivery changed dramatically at most colleges and universities. Because of transmission risks, institutions had to adjust from primarily face to face delivery to online or an online/face-to-face hybrid. Colleges and universities had to work quickly to build the infrastructure to deliver courses online that were typically taught face to face. The long-term effects of COVID-19 on classroom delivery have yet to play out, but it is reasonable to consider the potential for an increase in courses delivered in online or hybrid formats after the pandemic, as compared to before. You should be proactive when considering your options for course delivery, choosing delivery options that best fit your learning preferences. No matter how your courses are delivered, you should actively engage in all classes by participating in discussions, taking notes, and asking questions.

## Academic Success and Support Centers

Most colleges and universities offer academic support to students in the form of tutoring for specific subjects, academic coaching or mentoring, support for college-level writing, assistance with research, and the like. The organization of these services will vary from college to college. Some will house many or most services within an academic success center, whereas others (particularly larger schools) will have a series of support centers. For instance, your college or university might have a centralized center for tutoring and/or academic coaching, but a separate writing center. Another college might have a center that helps both with writing and research, whereas another might offer writing support alongside tutoring and expect students to go to the library for support in the research process. Some colleges offer tutoring within each academic department, but may have a central directory for those services. It is in your best interest to explore your college, its website, and the syllabi for classes you are taking, to learn where you can best access academic support when you need it.

> Be proactive! Access support before you need it! Make a habit of attending at least one support session (tutoring, coaching, mentoring, office hours, or review session) for each class you are taking. You'll grow more comfortable with student success services, and you can decide later, as you earn good grades in your courses, to let go of the supports you don't need.

### DISCOVERY

Where at my college or university can I seek academic support for the following areas?

Tutoring for mathematics _____

Tutoring for sciences _____

Tutoring for business courses _____

Tutoring for other kinds of courses I am taking _____

Assistance with writing _____

Support for academic research _____

Academic coaching or mentoring _____

# Career Centers

You may be thinking, "I'm new to college so I don't need to worry about visiting my university's Career Center until later." In some ways, you may be right, as Career Centers are generally more beneficial for junior and senior level students who are lining up internships, networking with employers, and learning how to negotiate salary. However, there are many ways Career Centers can benefit first-year and sophomore students as well, including researching career options tied to your major or expected major, learning how to build your resume and cover letter, developing interviewing skills, and getting connected to professional organizations. You can gain an advantage on your peers and future job competition by engaging with your institution's Career Center early in your college career.

> "I met with a Career Center counselor my freshman year to help with my résumé, which ended up helping me get a spot in an Emerging Scholars Program. I also used the Career Center to help prepare me for my interview for medical school. I ended up getting accepted, so I would say my experience with the Career Center was very beneficial to me."
>
> — Payton M., senior, Psychology

# University Registrar

A college or university registrar is the official record keeper of student and college records. Student records include official transcript information such as course grades, GPA, credits taken and earned, major, minor, and concentration information, and progress toward degree. University records kept by the registrar are vast and include academic policies, university calendars, and the university catalog.

## Student Records

As a new college student, you should become familiar with how to access your academic transcript. Your college or university registrar likely has an online version of your transcript that you can access to keep track of your progress toward graduation. While your academic advisor will help you identify classes and help you navigate your major, it is your responsibility to keep track of your own progress.

In Chapter 2, you learned how to set SMART goals that are specific, measurable, achievable, relevant and time-bound. Hopefully you have included a GPA goal among your SMART goals. You may have heard the saying that "C's get degrees." This may be true, in that a C will likely earn you credit for the course, and a transcript full of C's will typically result in a 2.0 GPA, meeting the minimum GPA graduation requirement. On the other hand, many employers will ask that you provide a copy of your college transcript, and a 2.0 GPA may not represent the standard of work they are looking for in new employees. A low GPA could make you less competitive in the workplace when compared to other applicants. When I hear students say "C's get degrees," I often respond with *"while C's may get degrees, they won't get you jobs."*

---

### DISCOVERY

1. Write or re-write your SMART goal for GPA this semester. (Refer back to Chapter 2 p 81 for a review of SMART goal setting)

   _____

   _____

   _____

---

Too frequently new first-year students do not take their classes and grades as seriously as they should, and they dig themselves a GPA hole during their first term. Research has shown that college students' first term is often their worst in terms of GPA, and a rough first term can contribute to their not returning to college. While a poor GPA during a single semester isn't likely to get you suspended from the university, it can put you on that path. Making a plan to achieve a high GPA during your first year of college will put you on a successful path toward graduating and being competitive in your field's job market.

Earning credits is also an important piece of the college puzzle. While withdrawing from a class may be an effective way of avoiding a low GPA, you should set a goal to complete every class you register for, so that you consistently earn credits toward your degree. Your class standing is determined by the credit hours you have earned, and not by the amount of time or number of semesters you have been enrolled in college courses, something many new college students do not understand. Higher class standing often carries benefits such as earlier registration, housing options, parking, access to events and athletics, and other opportunities. Most colleges use the following or similar guidelines to determine class standing:

| Credits earned | Class standing |
| --- | --- |
| 0–29 | Freshman/first-year |
| 30–59 | Sophomore |
| 60–89 | Junior |
| 90+ | Senior |

**DISCOVERY**

**Calculating Your Anticipated GPA Activity**

A quick internet search may yield you a GPA calculation tool where you can input your anticipated course grades and credit hours associated with those grades to see your anticipated term GPA. In the case you cannot find one online, you can use the formula below to calculate your GPA. You will want to make sure you find out your college or university's grade points before calculating your GPA.

$$\frac{(\text{Grade Point [GP] 1} \times \text{credit hours [CH] 1}) + (\text{GP 2} \times \text{CH 2}) + (\text{GP 3} \times \text{CH 3}) + (\text{GP 4} \times \text{CH 4}) - \text{until all classes are accounted for}}{\text{Total \# of Credits Attempted}}$$

Grade points are numerical values given to letter grades. Note that some institutions score "+" and "−" grades too so check your college or university's website for details. For this activity, you can use the following grade points to practice:

- "A" = 4.0
- "B" = 3.0
- "C" = 2.0
- "D" = 1.0
- "F" = 0.0

Example:

If you receive the following grades in a given term:

- "A" in Biology (4 credits)
- "B" in Art History (3 credits)
- "C" in English (3 credits)
- "D" in Math (3 credits)
- "F" in Introductory Engineering (1 credit)

Your GPA calculation formula will look like:

$$\frac{(4.0 \times 4) + (3.0 \times 3) + (2.0 \times 3) + (1.0 \times 3) + (0.0 \times 1)}{4 + 3 + 3 + 3 + 1}$$

$$\text{GPA} = 2.428$$

1. What is my anticipated GPA for the semester after utilizing the GPA calculation tool?

   _____

   _____

   _____

2. Were you surprised by the grades you need to earn in each class to achieve your SMART goal GPA?

   _____

   _____

   _____

3. Make a list of weekly choices you need to make to achieve your SMART goal GPA (e.g., review Biology 101 notes daily, complete History 101 reading assignments, complete Math 100 practice problems).

   _____

   _____

   _____

## University Catalog

Your college or university catalog contains all major and minor information, courses, enrichment programs, and academic policies at your university. You can search not only for the array of undergraduate and graduate programs offered by your institution, but also requirements for each, and descriptions for all courses your college offers. When you are looking for any sort of academic information, the college or university catalog is a great place to start.

**University Academic Progress Standards** Included in your college's catalog are academic expectations for continued enrollment at your institution. Colleges and universities have categories of academic progress that often include designations such as good standing, academic warning or difficulty, academic suspension, and academic expulsion. Each of these categories is associated with a particular GPA range, as well as credit completion and/or progress toward degree. Students who fall below good standing will typically face GPA and course completion requirements to regain good standing over the next term. For instance, at most 4-year colleges and universities, a standard for good academic standing is achieving at least a "C" average or 2.0 GPA. If you fall below that minimum requirement you are likely to go on academic warning or difficulty which often includes a GPA and credit hour completion progress requirement for the upcoming term. If you are already on academic warning and do not achieve the minimum progress standard you may be suspended from enrolling in at least the upcoming semester. Suspensions can be as brief as one semester or as long as multiple years. It is important that you know what your college's academic progress standards so that you avoid an unwelcome surprise.

### DISCOVERY

1. What are my college or university's academic progress standards?

   _____

   _____

   _____

## University Calendars

Your college or university registrar maintains the academic calendar which includes important dates such as course withdrawal deadlines, registration dates, final exam schedules, billing dates, and others. Making sure you know dates and deadlines is essential for giving yourself the opportunity to take actions necessary for your own academic success! The academic calendar will show you, for instance, your last day to withdraw from a class to avoid a poor grade on your transcript, when registration begins so you can register as early as possible and gain best access to courses and your preferred days and times to take those courses, and when final exams take place so you can plan and prepare ahead. An internet search should easily direct you to your college or university's academic calendar.

**DISCOVERY**

1.  What is the deadline to withdraw from a class? _____

2.  When are final exams? _____

*The Family Educational Rights and Privacy Act of 1974 (FERPA)* Commonly known as FERPA, the Family Educational Rights and Privacy Act requires colleges and universities accepting federal monies to protect the privacy of student information. What this usually means for college students is that unless you expressly give permission through a process your college or university has established, your college or university is legally unable to provide personally identifiable information such as your gender, race, ethnicity, religious affiliation, or pictures of you to anyone, including your parents. Your education records such as your grades, class schedule, transcripts, and disciplinary records are also protected and cannot be shared without your permission.

# Revisiting Material From Ch 1: Ready for Midterms

Remember in Chapter 1 where you got organized, analyzed your syllabi, developed a study plan, and created a weekly planner? Those steps were designed for you, to get you off to a solid start toward academic success in college. If you missed any of those steps, it's not too late to get started now! Go back to Chapter 1 to revisit those, and complete the end-of-chapter exercises. This is a good time to check in with yourself and see how those areas are working for you. Remember that these are part of a learning process, which means that you should expect to revisit them, evaluate how you are doing with them, and make adjustments as needed.

**DISCOVERY**

1. In terms of study space, where have you found that you study best? Is there anything you need to add to or subtract from your study space location or layout? Are there any other changes that will make your study more effective?

   _____

   _____

   _____

2. How are your homework or assignments going? Are you submitting all of your assigned work? Are you submitting it on time? Do you need to make adjustments to your schedule or your planner so that you don't miss submitting your work? If so, what adjustments can you make?

   _____

   _____

   _____

3. Are you clear about what is required of you in each class? Do you need to revisit the syllabus to make sure you understand and remember what is expected and how you will be evaluated in each class?

   _____

   _____

   _____

4. Is your weekly planner or calendar filled out with study time, assignments, projects, tests, and other classwork for the next 4 weeks? If not, this is the time to add those items to your planner or calendar.

   _____

   _____

   _____

5. Are you reading your textbook/materials before class, taking notes during class, and reviewing notes and materials after class? If not, now is the time to make those activities a priority, for academic success. How can you implement or continue this before-during-after study plan?

   _____

   _____

   _____

6. By now, it is likely that midterms are coming up soon. Are your midterm tests, projects or assignments listed in your calendar? Do you need to schedule extra study time in advance of midterms? (The answer is almost always "yes".)

_____

_____

_____

Go ahead and plan your extra time for midterm study and projects *now* by adding it to your planner. Follow these guidelines:

1. Begin studying for any midterm exam 5 to 7 days in advance. In other words, enter extra study sessions in your planner beginning a week before your exam. (If you are reading this and your first midterm is tomorrow, just begin where you are! Add extra study time to your planner starting today.)

2. Be specific about how you will study and what materials you will study. As an example, let's say you plan to study for your biology exam for 6 additional hours, broken into 3 study sessions of 2 hours each, during the week before the exam. Instead of entering "study for Biology midterm exam" in your planner for each session, you can be more efficient and effective by taking a few minutes to plan *how* and *what* you will study.

   • Your first study session could be "Review Biology chapters and notes for chapters 1 to 4."

   • Your second study session could be "Review Biology chapters and notes for chapters 5 to 8."

3. During your first couple of study sessions, make a "further study" list of concepts, processes and terms you found more difficult, or need to spend more time with.

   • Your third study session could be "Review concepts and terms on 'further study' list".

4. While you study, remember to take short breaks to refresh your mind and your body – move away from the table and stretch, walk a flight of stairs, go outside for a brief moment – and then get back into the study zone.

5. At the end of each study session, quiz yourself on the material, as if you were taking the test. Or, use flashcards and review questions that may be part of your textbook or related materials. If you study with a group, quiz each other, and try to explain concepts and processes to one another.

6. As you encounter concepts or terms you are not confident about, be proactive and schedule time to attend tutoring or speak with your professor or graduate assistant about your questions. This is where planning a week ahead can really help ensure you have time to access the resources you need.

7. Pro tip: Add one more study session the day before the exam to review all of your materials one more time. Then, get a good night of sleep the night before the exam, so you can approach it well-rested and energized.

"When I do have multiple exams, I make sure to allow myself an adequate amount of time to study for each exam. I love having a schedule but also like to make sure it is loose enough where I allow myself wiggle room for other activities and/or unexpected events. My hours spent studying varies based on the difficulty of each class. My best strategy for studying for midterms and exams in general is to try to reach out to students who have already taken the course. This can be helpful because you can get advice on what to study and more specifics about the exam itself (format/difficulty). Then, after reaching out to a former student, I personally spend my time continuously working problems and quizzing myself on the material I am about to be tested on. I am a hands-on learner and I learn a lot from repetition."

— Kenzie B., senior, Mechanical Engineering

# Financial Aid and Scholarships

## Forms of Aid

When it comes to paying for college, you should be informed about who is paying for your college experience and how this funding works, whether funding comes from yourself, your family members, merit-based scholarships, sponsoring organizations, loans, grants, or work-study. You can consult your college or university's financial aid office when you have questions or concerns about paying for college. It is no secret that college can be expensive, and that student loan debt is a significant consideration for college students nowadays. Being a smart college consumer can help you minimize your cost of attendance. Students who need assistance paying for college can apply for several different forms of financial aid, the term used to encompass all forms how students get help paying for college including scholarships, grants, loans, or Federal Work-Study.

Scholarships are typically "free money" that does not have to be paid back and are based on your history, talents, or area of study. You should apply for as many scholarships as you are eligible for through your college or university and private organizations. You should also know your institution's scholarship application deadline which is generally February or March of the academic year prior to when your scholarship begins. For example, the deadline for scholarships for classes beginning fall term 2025 are likely February or March, 2024. A quick internet search will yield you opportunities for scholarships that you may not have known existed.

© IhorZigor/Shutterstock.com

Federal grants, federal loans, and Federal Work Study are monies provided by the U.S. Federal Government. To apply for these, students must fill out the Free Application for Federal Student Aid, or FAFSA. As a high school student seeking federal financial aid, you or your parents would have already filled out a FAFSA for your first year in college. If you are seeking federal financial aid, you must fill out a FAFSA each year and should do so as soon as it becomes available, which is generally in October of the year prior to the academic year for which you are seeking aid (for example, apply in October 2021 for funding to cover the academic year 2022–2023). Like scholarships, grants are free money – but unlike scholarships, this money comes from the state or federal government. Federal Work Study allows students the opportunity to work on campus and receive an hourly wage but there are restrictions and not all students qualify. If you do qualify you should look for on-campus opportunities for part-time employment because as you will see below, part-time employment during college can be beneficial.

Student loans have to be paid back. Federal student loans are the most common form of student loan because they typically have the lowest interest rates. If you do not have enough funding through scholarships, grants, or your own (or your family's) savings, your first student loan choice should be federal. After you complete the FAFSA you will be provided a loan amount offer through your college or university that you will need to accept to receive. You can choose the amount to accept, and should choose the lowest amount needed to cover your immediate college expenses. Many times, students accept the full loan offer when they do not truly need that much funding, and as a result they end up with more student loan debt later. There are also private student loan vendors that you can find online, but they often carry higher interest rates and should serve only as a last resort.

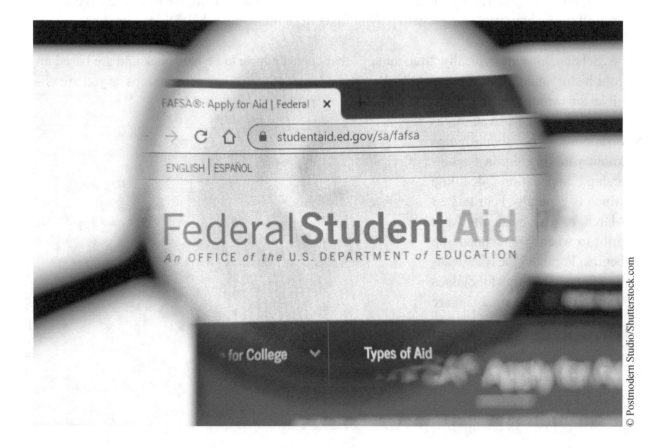

1. Provide your best estimate of how each method of payment is covering your student bill this semester. If you don't know, find out.

   a. Scholarships or Grants    $_____    % of total _____

   b. Student Loans    $_____    % of total _____

   c. Out of Pocket    $_____    % of total _____

## Credit Cards

Using credit allows you to purchase something now with a promise of paying it later. As a college student you may receive offers to apply for credit cards. Credit cards can be beneficial for building your credit history or useful in a monetary emergency but should be approached with caution. While having a credit card makes it easy to purchase a new outfit or a dinner for friends, you should avoid using it for those kinds of purchases. Credit cards come with high interest rates that can make it difficult to pay off your debt. Once you make a purchase, chances are you will be expected to pay it off within the next month or two with at least a 10% interest charge. It is not uncommon for students new to credit cards to get themselves into a large amount of credit card debt quickly. Like private student loans that are also high interest, you should avoid using your credit card except for emergencies and should consult with your family before applying for one.

## Being a Smart Consumer

Finding lower cost options for college essentials while avoiding nonessential costs is a good strategy. As a new college student, you likely do not have much experience making your own budget. Your college student budget would include housing, dining, textbooks and supplies, personal care, transportation, and other expenses. Most colleges and universities offer housing, dining, and parking options with significant cost differences. Smart college consumers make choices based on their current needs and avoid costing their families more money or themselves more future debt.

Being a smart college consumer may also mean taking classes during the summer at your local community college where cost of attendance is often much lower than 4-year universities. Many colleges and universities offer online tools for calculating your college costs, as well as online tools for maintaining a budget while in college. Be a smart consumer! Utilize these tools and be proactive with your college financial well-being, which can decrease your stress and allow you to focus on college success.

## Working While in College

Working during college is a necessity for some college students, and an option for others. A part-time job can help you reduce debt, provide spending money, and give you entry-level experiences in your field. According to research by the Department of Education, working during college can actually improve grades if full-time students who limit working to 12 hours or less per week. Data indicates that students who work part-time have improved grades because they are forced to manage their time, and they cultivate more self-discipline than students who are less busy. You should be cautious, however, as the same research indicates that working 15 or more hours per week can hurt students' grades. Like anything else, working a part-time job requires balance, as well as some degree of flexibility from your employer. You must be disciplined enough to schedule time for homework and study, and be able to avoid extra shifts that may negatively affect your grades.

## Accessibility Resource Centers

Accessibility resource centers' primary function is to provide academic accommodation resources for students in order to ensure equal opportunity to educational opportunities. Often still referred to as disability centers on college campuses, the most common function of these centers is to provide resources for students' cognitive or physical characteristics that may put them at a disadvantage for college success. These characteristics include visible disabilities like cerebral palsy, amputation or paralysis, as well as invisible disabilities such as hearing or vision loss, autism, ADHD, learning disabilities, mental health disorders, and chronic illness. If you had accommodations in high school such as extended test time, a designated note taker, or others, you should utilize your right to accommodations in college as well.

Unfortunately, many new college students want to flee the stigma of having a learning accommodation, so they choose to not utilize them, and as a result have unnecessary difficulty in their college classes. At the very least, you should access your accommodations to begin your college career. You can always make an informed decision to move away from accommodations later after you prove to yourself that you don't need them. Students should remember that information on learning accommodations is protected by federal law, and only faculty of the applicable course are notified so that they can work with you on the accommodations you need. Some college and university accessibility resource centers offer disability testing for students as well. It your responsibility to contact your college or university's accessibility resource center for accommodations you are entitled to have. They will not magically appear for you as they may have in high school, and your parents cannot access them for you in college either.

## Emotional Support or Counseling Centers

You should expect to experience stressors in college, whether they are related to college academics, social life, relationships, homesickness, loneliness, or others. Mental health awareness has been on the rise worldwide for some time now and on college campuses as well. Your college or university provides resources for you when you experience emotional challenges such as anxiety, stress, depression, sleep challenges, psychological challenges, and so on. Mental health and wellness services can include individual and group counseling, online coping resources, special workshops focusing on a specific challenge, wellness awareness, and more. Whether you have a history of emotional challenges or begin to experience them during college for the first time, you should take advantage of resources offered by your college or university's emotional support or counseling center.

## Gender and Multicultural Support Centers

As mentioned in Chapter 2, while gender and race themselves are not characteristics that put students at risk for not having college success, discrimination or a historical lack of resources that can be more prevalent in minority groups *are*. As a result, most colleges and universities offer both gender and racial diversity service centers that provide resources and a safe space for minority and other underserved populations. You can benefit from these centers if you feel a lack of community or belonging at your institution, or are interested in meeting others with similar experiences to your own. Often, these centers host cultural events and celebrations, lead informational or learning opportunities for those outside of the culture, provide mentorship opportunities, and offer skill development programming for community members. In addition, these centers can serve as a location for reporting gender or racially related discrimination or abuse.

## Student Health Centers

Student health centers provide basic health services for your college or university community that often include a pharmacy, immunization and vaccination access, sexual health services, nutrition services, x-rays, labs for illness testing, allergy services, and ambulance services. Some colleges and universities have fully-functioning hospitals on or next to campus as well. If you are not on your parent's health insurance, your college or university likely provides a health insurance option for you. Information on university health insurance policy options can be accessed at your student health center. You should expect to become ill at some point during your freshman year because you are in a new environment and are likely exposed to germs or allergens your body has not yet developed defenses to. When that happens, visit your college's health center for timely and appropriate medical care. We see many students fall behind each term because they got sick, did not seek medical care, and then stayed sick for weeks at a time. When it comes to your health, prioritize getting the care you need. Don't put it off!

## Recreation Centers

Unless you are attending an online college or university, your institution is likely to have a campus recreation center. These centers offer a variety of exercise equipment such as free weights, strength training equipment, treadmills, exercise bikes, and other cardiovascular equipment. Recreation centers can also offer basketball and racquetball courts, indoor tracks, climbing walls, and spaces for group exercise classes such as spin classes, yoga, or Pilates. Recreation centers often also provide personal training opportunities, as well as equipment rental that can range from basic equipment such as basketballs, yard games such as corn hole, or outdoor equipment such as bicycle, kayak, or climbing equipment rental. Additionally, many college recreation centers offer opportunities for you to participate in intramural or club sports teams and compete in campus-wide tournaments or even events versus other colleges or universities. If you are someone who likes to stay active or likes athletic competition, your campus recreation center has something for you.

## Chapter Summary

In this chapter, you learned about the kinds of supports and resources your college or university likely offers to ensure that you have a successful college experience, as well as a plan for your career. The end-of-chapter activities will give you the opportunity to dig deeper and see how these resources, and your own self-evaluation and planning, can keep you on track both in the short term (this semester or term) and in the long term (throughout your degree process and beyond). In Chapter 4, you will explore further how to engage with your college community socially, academically, and professionally.

## End-of-Chapter Activities

I.  **Create a midterm study plan for each class:**
  - Note in your planner the date and time of each midterm exam or project deadline.
  - Decide how many additional hours you need to devote to each subject to have a successful midterm experience.
  - Add those hours to your planner starting a week in advance of your exam or project, with specifics on how and what you plan to study or work on at each session.
  - Plan to study with others, whether by forming or joining a study group, or by attending tutoring or faculty office hours.
  - Add one more study and review session the day before the exam.

II. **Make A Monthly Budget.** Below is an example monthly budget. Notice the very first line provides space for calculating how much financial aid refund money you will have to spend each month. If you choose to receive a financial aid refund for a given term, it will arrive shortly after the semester begins. If you don't plan to receive a financial aid refund you can just skip that part of the budget activity and insert your income source(s) in the space provided.

## Example Monthly Budget

Financial Aid Refund for Term: $ <u>2,000</u> / Months in term: <u>4</u> = $ <u>500</u> spendable per month

| Income Source | Amount |
|---|---|
| Financial Aid refund for 1 month | 500 |
| Part-time job | 200 |
| Allowance from parents | 200 |
| | |
| Total | 900 |

| Expense | Goal | Actual |
|---|---|---|
| Rent | 500 | 500 |
| Utilities | 100 | 70 |
| Automobile expenses | 50 | 20 |
| Groceries | 100 | 50 |
| Cell phone | – | – |
| Grooming (haircut, etc.) | 50 | 20 |
| Entertainment | 100 | 125 |
| | | |
| Total | 900 | 785 |

Total Income $ 900
Minus total Expenses – $ 785
Total to Savings = $ 115

Now, create your own monthly budget. If you do not have an income source or expense already listed you can skip it. If you have other income sources or expenses list them instead.

## My Monthly Budget

Financial Aid Refund for Term: $_____ / Months in term: _____ = $_____ spendable per month

| Income Source | Amount |
|---|---|
| Financial Aid refund for 1 month | |
| Part-time job | |
| | |
| | |
| Total | |

| Expense | Goal | Actual |
|---|---|---|
| Rent | | |
| Utilities | | |
| Automobile expenses | | |
| Groceries | | |
| Cell phone | | |
| Grooming (haircut, etc.) | | |
| Entertainment | | |
| Miscellaneous | | |
| | | |
| | | |
| | | |
| | | |
| | | |
| | | |
| | | |
| Total | | |

Total Income          $_____
Total Expenses      − $_____
Total to Savings     = $_____

**III. University Service Scavenger Hunt:** find where to go for help and information. For each of the following topics or questions, use your college's website or other wayfinding materials to figure out where to get the help or information you need. Where do you go for each of the following? Enter the name of the office or department, and the building where they are located. Or, write down the name of their website, and their phone number.

| Learn about scholarships and financial aid | |
| --- | --- |
| Office: _____ | Department: _____ |
| Website: _____ | Phone No.: _____ |
| Location: _____ | |

| Speak with an advisor about what classes I should take | |
| --- | --- |
| Office: _____ | Department: _____ |
| Website: _____ | Phone No.: _____ |
| Location: _____ | |

| Register for classes | |
| --- | --- |
| Office: _____ | Department: _____ |
| Website: _____ | Phone No.: _____ |
| Location: _____ | |

| Purchase books and materials for my classes | |
| --- | --- |
| Office: _____ | Department: _____ |
| Website: _____ | Phone No.: _____ |
| Location: _____ | |

| Pay my student bill | |
| --- | --- |
| Office: _____ | Department: _____ |
| Website: _____ | Phone No.: _____ |
| Location: _____ | |

| See the academic calendar for this term | |
| --- | --- |
| Office: _____ | Department: _____ |
| Website: _____ | Phone No.: _____ |
| Location: _____ | |

| Find out my GPA | |
| --- | --- |
| Office: _____ | Department: _____ |
| Website: _____ | Phone No.: _____ |
| Location: _____ | |

| View my midterm grades or final grades | |
| --- | --- |
| Office: _____ | Department: _____ |
| Website: _____ | Phone No.: _____ |
| Location: _____ | |

| View my academic progress toward my degree | |
| --- | --- |
| Office: _____ | Department: _____ |
| Website: _____ | Phone No.: _____ |
| Location: _____ | |

**Get help with writing**

Office: _____    Department: _____

Website: _____    Phone No.: _____

Location: _____

**Get help with public speaking**

Office: _____    Department: _____

Website: _____    Phone No.: _____

Location: _____

**Get help finding resources for a research project**

Office: _____    Department: _____

Website: _____    Phone No.: _____

Location: _____

**Get tutoring for math-based or science-based courses**

Office: _____    Department: _____

Website: _____    Phone No.: _____

Location: _____

**Explore career paths**

Office: _____    Department: _____

Website: _____    Phone No.: _____

Location: _____

**Get help writing a resume**

Office: _____    Department: _____

Website: _____    Phone No.: _____

Location: _____

**Get mental health support or counseling**

Office: _____    Department: _____

Website: _____    Phone No.: _____

Location: _____

**See a doctor about an illness**

Office: _____    Department: _____

Website: _____    Phone No.: _____

Location: _____

**Learn about accommodations for my disability**

Office: _____    Department: _____

Website: _____    Phone No.: _____

Location: _____

**Learn about financial management**

Office: _____    Department: _____

Website: _____    Phone No.: _____

Location: _____

| Learn about Diversity, Equity and Inclusion at my college | |
|---|---|
| Office: _____ | Department: _____ |
| Website: _____ | Phone No.: _____ |
| Location: _____ | |

| Learn about support for gender diversity | |
|---|---|
| Office: _____ | Department: _____ |
| Website: _____ | Phone No.: _____ |
| Location: _____ | |

| Learn my college's policies for student conduct | |
|---|---|
| Office: _____ | Department: _____ |
| Website: _____ | Phone No.: _____ |
| Location: _____ | |

| Find a peer mentor | |
|---|---|
| Office: _____ | Department: _____ |
| Website: _____ | Phone No.: _____ |
| Location: _____ | |

| Receive academic coaching | |
|---|---|
| Office: _____ | Department: _____ |
| Website: _____ | Phone No.: _____ |
| Location: _____ | |

Now that you have compiled list of resource locations, go visit three of those resources in person (or if online, spend time perusing their website and social media). What did you learn from this experience?

I visited _____

I learned _____


I visited _____

I learned _____


I visited _____

I learned _____

## Chapter 4

# Engaging with Student Life Outside of the Classroom

| Choices of Successful Students | Choices of Struggling Students |
|---|---|
| 1. Actively engage in both in and out of the classroom opportunities. | 1. Do not actively engage in opportunities or do not attend at all. |
| 2. Explore themselves and how they fit in, then identify campus opportunities. | 2. Randomly select campus opportunities that do not fit their interests or personalities and lose interest in participating. |
| 3. Strive to gain a deeper understanding of themselves, their talents and motivations, while developing stronger empathy for others | 3. Do not attempt to understand themselves deeply, and are not open to understanding the perspectives and experiences of others. |
| 4. Get involved in outside-the-classroom opportunities such as university events, clubs or programs, the first-year experience, student government, and opportunities within their residential communities. | 4. Travel home over the weekends and do not engage with their campus communities. |
| 5. Continue to assess personal wellness, setting new goals each month or rethinking previous goals not yet achieved. | 5. Abandon personal wellness goals due to lack of investment, frustration, overwhelm or lack of focus. |

## Introduction

You may have participated in orientation or first-week activities in which you became familiar with student organizations, clubs, affinity groups, and extracurriculars at your college or university. If you jumped in at the start and are already connected, fantastic! If not, it's not too late to get on board. Either way, this chapter is an opportunity to dig deeper into the full student life experience offered where you are, and to plan ahead for the next 4 years.

### Focus Questions:

1. What outside-the-classroom opportunities does your college or university provide for its students?
2. What is the difference between active engagement and attendance?

## Finding Your Hidden Potential

You are probably familiar with Hans Christian Anderson's famous story "The Ugly Duckling" in which a young duckling is considered to be an outcast because of its difference in appearance.

One day the duckling grows up in to a beautiful swan and is accepted by its peers. This story provides the useful life lesson of not judging yourself or others by initial appearance, and instead searching for strengths and talents that may at first be unrecognizable, or not visible on the surface.

There are few places in society that provide such a diverse collection of self-exploration in one place as a college or university campus. As a result, you have opportunities that you did not have before, regardless of your background. Your college campus provides a network of entertainment, social, connection, advocacy, service, diversity and inclusion, and leadership opportunities that will help you discover your own path, but also improve your sense of belonging, satisfaction, and success in college and in life. The question is, will you take advantage of these opportunities?

# Knowing Yourself / How You Fit In ⊛

Research on student engagement and persistence demonstrates that there is a strong and positive correlation between a student's engagement in college life (e.g., co-curricular and extracurricular activities, clubs and organizations, or affinity groups) and their persistence, or the likelihood that they will remain in college until graduation. This is part of the reason we strongly encourage students to get connected and get involved in their college environments and organizations. The other reason, more directly, is that we want you to feel you are a member of the college or university you attend, to feel you know your classmates, professors, and administrators. While you learned about communication with faculty, advisors and others in earlier chapters, this one focuses the social learning (in addition to academics) that contributes to a holistic college experience and to your formation as a well-rounded, socially aware and empowered individual.

Part of getting involved at college is knowing who you are, and what your own interests are. These may still be coming into focus for you, particularly if this is your first time living on your own or your first time in a college environment. Your college may offer groups, clubs, ideas and opportunities that you haven't even heard of before! It may also represent the chance to get more involved in some things you have been curious about for a long time.

There are many personality tests available online, and the one we will use for this chapter, found at 16personalities.com, is based on the Myers-Briggs Type Indicator, or MBTI. Research on college students has shown important correlations between preferred learning style (covered in Chapter 5) and your MBTI personality profile, and there are also valuable connections to be drawn between personality type and student engagement. Understanding yourself through the MBTI has been shown in leadership and educational settings to have a positive impact on your relationships with others, and a more profound understanding of others in your community or on your team. While your personality type does not limit your capabilities, understanding yourself through this lens may help you make more informed decisions about "good fit" extracurriculars as well as areas you may wish to intentionally grow or cultivate.

## DISCOVERY

1.  If you could describe yourself in 5 words, what would they be? Try it below:

    _____

    _____

    _____

2.  Now, navigate to *16personalities.com* and take the personality test. On the results page, click to read the full description provided in the section labeled "Introduction." In the reflection below, you will refer to your personality inventory results. Note: you can enter your email address on the site to have a copy of your results sent to you.
    a.  My personality inventory results are (for instance, INTP-A, or ESFJ-T)_____

3.  After reading the basic type description (Introduction), which ideas or statements describe me the best?

    _____

    _____

    _____

Knowing even a little about personality types can help you understand yourself better as well as appreciate the ways in which others are different from you, strengthening your empathy and understanding of others in your community. It can also help you develop your own roadmap for success, based on your strengths, abilities and affinities. As you proceed through this chapter, keep in mind that you possess particular gifts, a unique view of the world, and a presence that literally nobody else can bring. We challenge you to consider what you could gain and learn by engagement in various aspects of student life, but also the individual spark that you add to the mix. As you choose clubs, extracurriculars and service organizations, don't underestimate your own potential to have a positive impact on others in your community. College is the time to try new things! Student life and student engagement can be the perfect way to do just that.

# Active Engagement

Engagement can be defined as how you participate in educationally effective practices, or practices that fit within the mission or values of the university. On a personal level, though, engagement is about your participation in the many academic, social and personal-developmental opportunities provided by your college or university, and your connection to others in your academic community. Engagement opportunities take place both inside and outside the classroom, and can be academic, social, or personal. Engagement opportunities may be diverse or varied, but one thing that is consistent across all of them is that *the level of engagement you experience is dependent on the amount of time and energy you invest in the activity.* Here is an example of students participating in a math tutoring session: An actively engaged student follows along with the tutor while she completes problems on the board, asks questions of the tutor, and completes practice problems as recommended by the tutor. A student who is not actively engaged in the same tutoring session may be posting on social media while the tutor is working through practice problems, afraid to ask questions, and skips recommended practice problems. It goes without saying that the actively engaged student is more likely to do well in their math class than the other student. While attendance is important, engagement is the key to success.

The same rules for engagement apply for nonacademic opportunities that your college or university provides. If you actively engage in a residence hall meeting or social event, put on by your college or university's student life office, you are more likely to get something out of it. Instead of just showing up, take advantage of opportunities by actively participating. If you do, research indicates that you have a much higher likelihood of staying in college and graduating on time. Research also indicates that active engagement can lead to gains, benefits, and outcomes in the following domains:

- cognitive and intellectual skill development
- college adjustment
- moral and ethical development
- practical competence and skills transferability
- accrual of social capital
- psychosocial development, productive racial and gender identity formation, and positive images of self

> "There are lots of ways to get involved on campus, literally hundreds of student organizations that range from 100+ members to a dozen members, so there is something for everyone. I don't think it's ever too late to get involved, but I would recommend starting your freshman year. The earlier you get involved, the more chances and opportunities you'll get to meet new people, make new friends, and do some things that you're interested in."
>
> – Cody H., senior majoring in Aerospace Engineering

1.  Identify and reflect on a time you actively engaged in an outside-the-classroom opportunity in high school or other previous educational experience. What did you do in order to actively engage, and what did you get out of the experience?

    _____

    _____

    _____

2.  Identify and reflect upon a time you were in attendance at a class, activity or event, but did not engage actively. What was the cause of your distraction? What did you get out of the experience?

    _____

    _____

    _____

# Opportunities for Active Engagement Outside of the Classroom

## Campus Events

Your college or university offers a variety of social and entertainment opportunities to help you let loose and have some fun! Campus events are a safe and fun way to relieve stress and meet new friends, and they can help you build connections to the university community. For example, your college or university may host tailgate parties, movies, carnivals, concerts, celebrations, or other campus-wide events. Often these events are free of cost and offer free giveaways and refreshments. Rather than traveling home every weekend to hang out with old friends, take advantage of events on your campus and within your college community. Students who attend college events report higher levels of satisfaction, belonging, and connection with their university community.

> "For me, the most fun and meaningful involvement experiences are the athletic events on campus. I've never felt more connected to my college peers than when sitting in the student section at the stadium or the coliseum. Even though I sat with friends, I still met new people and made new connections at almost every game. Athletic events gave me a sense of belonging because in those moments, it doesn't seem like there are thousands of other students that you don't know – it seems like you have thousands of friends cheering for your team."
>
> – Cody H., senior, Aerospace Engineering

© Piotr Piatrouski/Shutterstock.com

© Sean Locke Photography/Shutterstock.com

## Student Clubs and Organizations

Your college or university also offers university sponsored clubs and organizations for all kinds of student interests and hobbies. These clubs and organizations are generally student-led and in many cases were established by students seeking peers with similar interests. Clubs and organizations can be for academics, entertainment, advocacy, culture, sports or exercise, political viewpoints, service, or professional development. College organizations are a safe and fun way to relieve stress, meet new friends, and help build satisfaction with your college experience. Joining a club or organization can be a great way to develop skill sets, build your resume, or try something new!

> "My freshman year, I went to my university's "get on board day" which was a great way to get connected to people and different organizations on campus. For me, participating in large events sponsored by our Black Student Union were really important and fun experiences as a black woman attending a predominately white institution. Attending these events made me feel connected to my race in a way I didn't think was possible. Also, during my freshman year I began my minor within a Liberal Arts Living-Learning Community on my campus. This program engaged my mind and opened me up to different ways of thinking and beliefs. There, I found a community who may not always agree with the beliefs that I had but they respected them."
>
> – Eryn C., senior, Dance

## First-Year Experience

Your college or university has a first-year experience office tasked with helping first-year students get connected academically and socially through a variety of structured programs and events. First-Year Experience programming support the mission or values of the university, and oftentimes address needs of its first-year student body such as connecting to the university culture and traditions, providing leadership or mentoring opportunities, diversity development, and other opportunities for student growth. If you would like support getting connected to peers and your college or university, check out your college's First-Year Experience office.

## Student Government

Your college or university has a student government whose purpose is to represent the student body in discussions with campus leadership on policies that will affect them. Student government representatives are elected by their peers and carry important leadership roles at the university, frequently meeting with campus leaders such as faculty, department heads, deans, vice presidents, and even the university president. Student governments also lead and promote initiatives and events important to their constituents or helpful for their development. Student governments provide outlets for students to voice their concerns. If you are interested in leadership opportunities that can directly impact your college or university and your peers, check out your college or university's student government.

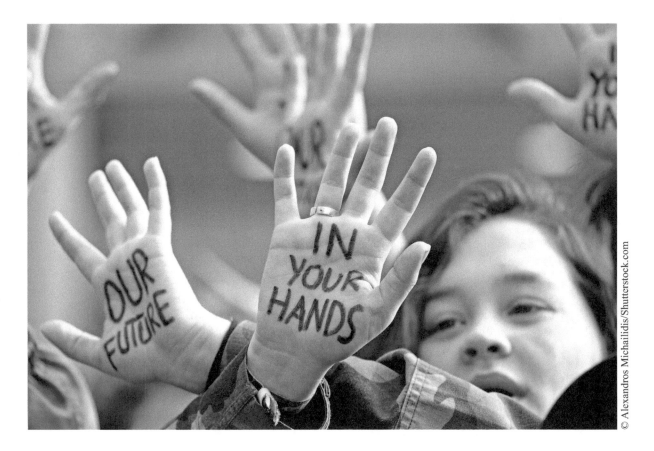

© Alexandros Michailidis/Shutterstock.com

## Residential Experience

Your residence community is much more than just the place that you sleep, relax, and hang out with friends. It offers engagement options such as events, programs, and leadership opportunities as well. In addition to the campus-wide events mentioned earlier, your residence hall and student organizations will likely host frequent smaller-group gatherings for meals, games, and other social activities. These programs follow the mission of the university and can be for the purpose of entertainment, building community, student development, and addressing particular student needs or desires. In addition, your residential community is likely to offer an opportunity for you to voice your concerns or take on a leadership opportunity through a residence hall association. Your residential community may also provide part-time job opportunities as a desk assistant or residential assistant (RA) that may include a wage or housing stipend so that you have a discounted or even free housing rate! It is important to get connected in your residence hall experience by attending floor or building meetings so that you are aware of important announcements or other information as well as opportunities the residential community provides.

## Service Opportunities

Your college or university probably has an office dedicated to providing service to the campus and/or surrounding community that you can join. Service experiences can include helping at local community centers, schools, nursing homes, food pantries, pet adoption agencies, park cleanup, or others. Service can be as short as just an hour or two or week-long or semester-long commitments. Participating in service opportunities not only help the local community but can also lead to these additional benefits:

- Personal and interpersonal development
- Leadership and communication skills
- Reduction of stereotypes and better cultural and racial understanding
- Sense of social responsibility and citizenship
- Satisfaction

"My favorite organization that I joined my freshman year was one where we mentored local elementary-school children. I really enjoyed the one-on-one interaction with students, helping them with homework, and doing fun activities with them. It was a great way to destress from college and really focus on being in the moment with the child you are mentoring. This organization has helped me feel part of the wider community – the elementary schools we visit are all off of campus, and I met a lot of community people through this program. It was nice to know that we all had the same goal in mind. . .the kids. Later, as a junior, I joined Volunteers Around the World. This organization goes on medical mission trips to impoverished countries and provides basic medical care. I really love the mission of this group and it tied a lot of my interests together, such as travel, medicine, and service."

– Jordan S., senior, Public Health

"Although I joined a lot of organizations my freshman year and was involved in lots of programs, I was constantly looking for one where I fit in the most. I finally found this after I joined my college's robotics team, in addition to professional organizations like the American Institute of Chemical Engineers and the Society of Women Engineers. The robotics team was the most fun and meaningful to me my first year because I had always wanted be involved in robotics but I had no knowledge about it. In this organization, I got to build my skills from scratch and grow as a person. We went on lots of field trips and I learned how to build and operate a drone! Later, I joined an organization in which I mentored high school and middle school students, which was my first opportunity to experience life outside of campus. I worked with these future college students to encourage them toward achieving their goals. Within my department, I was able to start doing outside-of-class research during my junior year. This sharpened and defined my next step in life, gave me important experiences, helped me build my resume and was the most fun I have ever had. Don't ever think it's too late to try something new."

– Oreoluwa A., senior, Chemical Engineering

## Chapter Summary

The story of the Ugly Duckling effectively characterizes how we all have great talents, strength, and beauty within each of us that may be at first unrecognizable. While many of your talents and strengths have already been recognized, many more may exist that your college community can help you discover and access. The college environment will offer a remarkable breadth of opportunities for self-exploration and active engagement, more than almost any other place in society. Taking advantage of and actively engaging in outside-the-classroom events, clubs, and programs can help you not only discover new things about yourself, but also build community, develop new skill sets, and improve your sense of belonging and satisfaction with your college experience.

## End-of-Chapter Activities

**I. Personality Inventory Revisit.** For a deeper dive into the personality inventory, return to your personality inventory results at *16personalities.com*. Once you have navigated back to the "Introduction" section, you will see a menu of additional sections on the left-hand side of the page. Navigate to "Strengths and Weaknesses." As you read about strengths and weaknesses of your type, which strengths do you think best describe you? How can you use those strengths powerfully toward your academic success and/or your engagement in student life in college?

_____

_____

_____

Now, which weaknesses do you think are most real for you? Name three academic habits or student engagement activities that you think could help you balance or address some of those weaknesses.

_____

_____

_____

As you keep clicking through the material related to your type at *16personalities.com*, you will see information devoted to Romantic Relationships, Friendships, Parenthood, Career, and Workplace Habits. Choose one or more of those to explore in greater depth. How do you think you will be able to use your particular traits and strengths in relationships with others and/or at work?

_____

_____

_____

## II. Engage with a Campus event, Club, or Program.

1. What is the name of the event, club, or program?

   _____

   _____

   _____

2. What was the mission of the event you attended?

   _____

   _____

   _____

3. How did you actively engage?

   _____

   _____

   _____

4. Will you engage again? Please explain.

   _____

   _____

   _____

**III. Academic Check-In.** Use the following academic check-in to determine how well you are actively engaging in the classroom. Circle the statement that best represents your current practices

| | | |
|---|---|---|
| 1. | Attend class | Always \| Sometimes \| Rarely \| Never |
| 2. | Arrive to class on time | Always \| Sometimes \| Rarely \| Never |
| 3. | Bring all appropriate materials to class (e.g., textbook, homework, binder, pen/pencil) | Always \| Sometimes \| Rarely \| Never |
| 4. | Keep attention on instructor during a lecture | Always \| Sometimes \| Rarely \| Never |
| 5. | Take good notes during a lecture | Always \| Sometimes \| Rarely \| Never |
| 6. | Ask questions when I have them | Always \| Sometimes \| Rarely \| Never |
| 7. | Stay awake through the entire class | Always \| Sometimes \| Rarely \| Never |
| 8. | Contribute to class discussions | Always \| Sometimes \| Rarely \| Never |
| 9. | Complete an equal share of responsibilities in small group discussions or assignments | Always \| Sometimes \| Rarely \| Never |
| 10. | Complete all assignments | Always \| Sometimes \| Rarely \| Never |
| 11. | Complete all expected readings | Always \| Sometimes \| Rarely \| Never |
| 12. | Turn in assignments on time | Always \| Sometimes \| Rarely \| Never |
| 13. | Check my phone during class | Always \| Sometimes \| Rarely \| Never |
| 14. | Take a bathroom break when I don't need to | Always \| Sometimes \| Rarely \| Never |
| 15. | Talk to peers when instruction is taking place | Always \| Sometimes \| Rarely \| Never |
| 16. | Daydream | Always \| Sometimes \| Rarely \| Never |

Successful students most often check "always" for numbers 1 to 12, and "rarely" or "never" for numbers 13 to 16.

Now, identify a statement from numbers 1 to 12 that you did not select "always" that you can commit to improving. How can you do so?

_____

_____

_____

## IV.  Wellness Check.

WELLNESS CHECK

Use the following wellness check-in to determine how you are doing in terms of self-care. Circle the statement that best represents your current practices

| | |
|---|---|
| – I avoid sugary beverages such as sweetened coffee/tea, sodas, and juices | Always \| Sometimes \| Rarely \| Never |
| – I limit my consumption of alcohol and mind-altering substances | Always \| Sometimes \| Rarely \| Never |
| – I am mindful of caloric intake when eating out | Always \| Sometimes \| Rarely \| Never |
| – I eat at least 5 fruits and vegetables per day OR I fill half my plate with fruits and veggies at every meal | Always \| Sometimes \| Rarely \| Never |
| – I bike or walk to class or work | Always \| Sometimes \| Rarely \| Never |
| – I do something physically active during quick study breaks | Always \| Sometimes \| Rarely \| Never |
| – I workout or play a sport regularly | Always \| Sometimes \| Rarely \| Never |
| – I notice when my body is showing signs that I am stressed or anxious | Always \| Sometimes \| Rarely \| Never |
| – I take steps to alleviate stress when I am feeling stressed or anxious | Always \| Sometimes \| Rarely \| Never |
| – I do deep breathing or meditation on a daily basis | Always \| Sometimes \| Rarely \| Never |
| – I have friends and/or family I can talk to regularly, who help lower my feelings of stress or anxiety | Always \| Sometimes \| Rarely \| Never |
| – I try to do something that makes me happy every day | Always \| Sometimes \| Rarely \| Never |
| – I give myself an hour to relax and wind down before bed | Always \| Sometimes \| Rarely \| Never |
| – I keep my bed as a sleep-only (not study and work) zone | Always \| Sometimes \| Rarely \| Never |
| – I sleep 7 to 8 hours each night | Always \| Sometimes \| Rarely \| Never |
| – I keep my room cool during sleep hours | Always \| Sometimes \| Rarely \| Never |

Which elements of your self-care are going really well? Which were points of focus over the past month, which have improved since your last check-in? Which ones are not going so well? Build on your progress by choose one or two new points that you wish to improve on and commit to those for the next 3 weeks. You could even create a SMART goal for them! At the end of 3 weeks, you will likely find that they have become easy and habitual for you.

If you did not fully accomplish your goals from the last check-in, you could also recommit to those goals. In that case, take the time to analyze why you did not succeed at those goals last time – were they too broad or nonspecific? Were they not realistic or achievable? Once you have identified the issues, reframe or reconstruct your goals to make them SMARTer (specific, measurable, achievable, relevant, and time-bound). Then, try again for a month, starting now!

Above all, be kind and understanding to yourself. Wellness goals are intended to help you take good care of yourself, not to give you a reason to feel badly about how you are doing. Remember that personal wellness is a journey, and we all run into bumps in the road. When you hit a bump, determine what happened without judging yourself harshly, and then consider what will most help you move toward better self-care.

# References

Anaya, G. (1996). College experiences and student learning: The influence of active learning, college environments, and cocurricular activities. *Journal of College Student Development, 37*(6), 611–622.

Astin, A. W. (1993). *What matters in college? Four critical years revisited.* Jossey-Bass.

Baxter Magolda, M. B., & King, P. M. (Eds.). (2004). *Learning partnerships: Theory and models of practice to educate for self-authorship.* Stylus.

Bean, J. P. (1990). Why students leave: Insights from research. In D. Hossler & J. P. Bean (Eds.), *The strategic management of college enrollments* (pp.147–169). Jossey-Bass.

Bean, J. P. (2005). Nine themes of college student retention. In A. Seidman (Ed.), *College student retention: Formula for student success* (pp. 215–244). ACE and Praeger.

Cabrera, A. F., Nora, A., Terenzini, P. T., Pascarella, E. T., & Hagedorn, L. S. (1999). Campus racial climate and the adjustment of students to college: A comparison between White students and African American students. *The Journal of Higher Education, 70*(2), 134–202. https://doi: 10.2307/2649125

Dettlaff, A. J. (2006). Personality type preferences of social work students: Enhancing the educational process through self-awareness and understanding of personality variables. *Journal of Baccalaureate Social Work, 11*(2), 1–23. https://doi.org/10.18084/1084-7219.11.2.88

Dunning, D. (1999). *Introduction to type and communication.* Consulting Psychologists Press.

Evans, N. J. (1987). A framework for assisting student affairs staff in fostering moral development. *Journal of Counseling and Development, 66,* 191–193.

Evans, N. J., Forney, D. S., & Guido-DiBrito, F. (1998). *Student development in college: Theory, research, and practice.* Jossey-Bass.

Harper, S. R. (2008). Realizing the intended outcomes of Brown: High-achieving African American male undergraduates and social capital. *American Behavioral Scientist 51*(7), 1–24.

Harper, S. R., & Quaye, S. J. (2007). Student organizations as venues for Black identity expression and development among African American male student leaders. *Journal of College Student Development, 48*(2), 133–159.

Harper, S. R. & Quaye, S. J. (2015). Making engagement equitable for students in U.S. higher education. In S. J. Quaye & S. R. Harper (Eds.), *Student engagement in higher education: Theoretical perspectives and practical approaches for diverse populations* (2nd ed.). Routledge.

Herbster, D. L., & et al. (1996). *Comparing university students and community college students learning styles and Myers-Briggs Type Indicator (MBTI) preferences.* Paper presented at the Annual Meeting of the Association of Teacher Educators.

Jean, F. E. (2019). *Transformational leadership for the helping professions: Engaging head, heart, and soul.* Oxford University Press.

Kuh, G. D., Palmer, M., & Kish, K. (2003). The value of educationally purposeful out-of-class experiences. In T. L. Skipper & R. Argo (Eds.), *Involvement in campus activities and the retention of first-year college students.* The First-Year Experience Monograph Series (No.36, pp. 19–34). University of South Carolina, National Resource Center for the First-Year Experience and Students in Transition.

Murphy, L., Eduljee, N. B., Croteau, K., & Parkman, S. (2020). Relationship between personality type and preferred teaching methods for undergraduate college studnents. *International Journal of Research in Education and Science, 6*(1), 100–109.

Myers, S. (2016). The five functions of psychological type. *Journal of Analytical Psychology, 61*(2), 183–202. https://doi.org/10.1111/1468-5922.12205

Pascarella, E. T., & Terenzini, P. T. (2005). *How college affects students: A third decade of research.* Jossey-Bass.

Pearson, N. G., & DeFrank-Cole, L. (2017). Who is taking our classes? A single-institution study of leadership student personality types. *Journal of Leadership Education, 16*(3), 34.

Quaye, S. J., & Harper, S. R. (2014). *Student engagement in higher education: Theoretical perspectives and practical approaches for diverse populations* (2nd ed.). Routledge.

Quenk, N. (2009). *Essentials of Myers-Briggs Type Indicator Assessment* (2nd ed.). John Wiley & Sons, Inc.

Tinto, V. (1993). *Leaving college: Rethinking the causes and cures of student attrition* (2nd ed.). University of Chicago Press.

Tinto, V. (1996). Reconstructing the first year of college. *Planning for Higher Education, 25,* 1–6.

Tinto, V. (1997). Colleges as communities: Exploring the educational character of student persistence. *Journal of Higher Education, 68*(6), 599–623.

Tinto, V. (2000). Taking retention seriously: Rethinking the first year of college. *NACADA Journal, 19*(2), 5–10.

Torres, V., Howard-Hamilton, M. F., & Cooper, D. L. (2003). *Identity development of diverse populations: Implications for teaching and administration in higher education. ASHE-ERIC Higher Education Report* (Vol. 29, No. 6). Jossey-Bass.

Tross, S. A., Harper, J. P., Osher, L. W., & Kneidinger, L. M. (2001). Not just the usual cast of characteristics: Using personality to predict college performance and retention. *Journal of College Student Development, 41*(3), 325–336.

## Chapter 5

# Building your Success Toolkit

| Choices of Successful Students | Choices of Struggling Students |
|---|---|
| 1. Cultivate a growth mindset and resilience, and choose to learn from their setbacks. | 1. Cultivate a fixed mindset and believe that their setbacks define them. |
| 2. Constantly evaluate which study habits and personal habits are and are not effective, and make changes as needed. | 2. Keep doing the same thing in their academic and personal lives, whether or not it is really working for them. |
| 3. Take notes during class, using a note-taking strategy that suits both them and the class content. | 3. Fail to take notes during class, or take notes that later do not make sense or are not very helpful for study. |
| 4. Review notes after class, following up on any questions that arise. | 4. Fail to review notes after class. |
| 5. Practice active listening in the classroom so they hear and understand what their professor and classmates are really saying. | 5. Listen carelessly or don't really listen to what their professor and classmates are saying. |
| 6. Take notes on assigned readings. Employ active reading strategies to better understand important and difficult readings. | 6. Fail to take notes on readings. Read in an unfocused way and as a result don't remember very much of what they read. |
| 7. Set aside time to prepare each day beginning several days before a test or exam. | 7. Cram for tests and exams at the last minute. |
| 8. Prepare intelligently for tests by finding out as much as possible about test format and style in advance. | 8. Go into a test or exam with no idea about its format or content. |

## Introduction

Have you ever heard the adage that genius is 1% inspiration and 99% perspiration? In this chapter, you will learn how to further develop and hone your academic skills (the "perspiration" part of that equation) for success in your college classes. You will also learn how to cultivate self-empathy and a growth mindset, powerful tools to help you focus on what and how you are learning, even when failures or setbacks occur. Your mindset and your study skills are a powerful combination that, developed appropriately, can set you on the path to success in college.

### Focus Questions:

1. What is the Growth Mindset, and how can you use it for college success?
2. What are some next-level study skill techniques?

Genius is one percent INSPIRATION ninety-nine percent PERSPIRATION

© Tri Yuli Astuti/Shutterstock.com

## Developing Self-Empathy and a Growth Mindset

In *Dare to Lead*, Brené Brown identifies empathy as one of the essential skills needed to navigate the world successfully. In her definition of empathy, she includes self-empathy or self-compassion. She encourages her readers to be warm and understanding toward themselves when they fail to meet their goals or when they feel inadequate, giving this advice: "talk to yourself the way you'd talk to someone you love." (p. 158). If we could encourage our students to cultivate one habit, this would be *the one*, because when you choose to think and act with self-compassion and self-care, you are infinitely more able to understand your failures as learning experiences, to build yourself back up, and to keep working on your tasks with curiosity and motivation. A self-compassionate or self-empathetic response helps you understand yourself as someone who is constantly learning, growing and changing.

---

**DISCOVERY**

1. Think of a time when you failed at something. If you were going to talk to yourself compassionately about this experience the way you would talk to a close friend or family member, what would you say? How do you feel when you consider this empathetic response to yourself?

   _____

   _____

   _____

---

In Chapter 6, you will learn about resilience, or your ability to adapt to stressful situations over time. Growth mindset forms part of the foundation for your resilience, so we'll discuss it here.

Carol Dweck, a pioneering researcher in the field of educational psychology, has dedicated her career to understanding how students' mindsets affect how they learn. She has defined a growth mindset as the belief that your personal characteristics, including intellectual abilities and talents, can be grown and developed. She has defined a fixed mindset, on the other hand, as the belief that these characteristics are fixed and unchangeable. Research by Carol Dweck and others has proven that the way students think about themselves and their own abilities affects not only how they feel, but also whether they are likely to learn new skills, develop new habits and achieve their goals. *People who cultivate a growth mindset are more likely to thrive when faced with challenges or even failures, and they continue to improve. On the other hand, people who hold more of a fixed mindset are more likely to avoid challenges and to give up when faced with failure, thereby not meeting their potential.* Research on mindsets has continued to show, even in the face of significant worldwide challenges, that growth mindsets help students succeed. Studies of college students during the COVID-19 pandemic have shown that growth mindset was essential to students' ability to cope and contributed significantly to their academic success during a period of worldwide crisis. Most importantly for your success in college, growth mindset is directly related to your ability to engage in active learning, and to face the complexity of your college environment with courage and flexibility.

## DISCOVERY

1. In what ways am I courageous? In what ways am I flexible? How do I demonstrate these characteristics in my college studies?

   _____

   _____

   _____

2. Use the chart below to test your own Growth Mindset. For each question, circle the number that best describes you. Then, total and record your score.

   _____

   _____

   _____

|  | Strongly Agree | Agree | Disagree | Strongly Disagree |
|---|---|---|---|---|
| Your intelligence is something basic about you that you cannot change very much. | 0 | 1 | 2 | 3 |
| No matter how much intelligence you have, you can always change it quite a bit. | 3 | 2 | 1 | 0 |

| | Strongly Agree | Agree | Disagree | Strongly Disagree |
|---|---|---|---|---|
| You can learn new things, but you cannot change your basic intelligence. | 0 | 1 | 2 | 3 |
| The harder you work at something, the better you will be. | 3 | 2 | 1 | 0 |
| I often get angry or hurt when I get feedback about my performance. | 0 | 1 | 2 | 3 |
| I appreciate when people, parents, coaches or teachers give me feedback about my performance. | 3 | 2 | 1 | 0 |
| Truly smart people do not need to try hard. | 0 | 1 | 2 | 3 |
| You can always change how talented you are. | 3 | 2 | 1 | 0 |
| You are born with the talents you have, and not much is really going to change that. | 0 | 1 | 2 | 3 |
| An important reason I do my schoolwork is that I enjoy learning new things. | 3 | 2 | 1 | 0 |

Total _____
Score chart:
22–30    Strong Growth Mindset
17–21    Growth Mindset with some Fixed Ideas
11–16    Fixed Mindset with some Growth Ideas
0–10     Strong Fixed Mindset

*Adapted from: Dweck, C. S. (2006). *Mindset: The new psychology of success*. New York: Random House Inc.

After taking the mindset quiz, and scoring yourself, where did you fall in terms of fixed versus growth mindset?

_____

_____

_____

**Growth Mindset:** If you scored more strongly in favor of a growth mindset, this means that you believe that effort and practice can help you master even difficult material. It also means that you see failure as a temporary setback, that you persist in your goals, and that you see feedback as an opportunity to grow.

**Fixed Mindset:** If you scored more strongly in favor of a fixed mindset, this means that you believe talent and intelligence are qualities you are born with (or not), and that effort and practice are not likely to help very much. It also means that you may see temporary setbacks as personal failures, and that you may experience feedback as a personal attack.

Do you think your score is an accurate reflection of your current beliefs regarding fixed mindset and growth mindset? Why or why not?

_____

_____

_____


Regardless of your current outlook on talent and intelligence, anyone can cultivate a growth mindset, which includes the resilience to learn from failures, the persistence to keep working toward your goals, and the willingness to build your abilities. The good news for college students is that growth mindset has been correlated with increased academic success, and also with increased enjoyment of academic tasks. *Once you can take a position of curiosity and willingness to learn, and let go of your own negative self-perceptions, you will likely find that the experience of learning is more satisfying and enjoyable.*

© Photo wali sark/Shutterstock.com

# Next-Level Academic Skills

Now that we have explored self-empathy and mindset, let's take a deeper dive into some of the academic skills you have begun to practice in your college classes. This is an opportunity for you to learn, practice, and get better at the college-level study habits you have begun to implement.

You may find that in your college or university classes you are faced with a totally new set of expectations about your ability to learn independently by reading and attending lectures. Some students make this transition easily, but some do not. The difference between these two groups is not native intelligence, but *preparation*. If you find yourself in the first group, it is likely that you have already learned the more mature study strategies that allow you to analyze and define your assigned learning tasks. You may have also learned to choose the study strategies that are most effective for those tasks, and to check and adjust your study strategies as you go along. If you find yourself struggling with college-level study, it's because you have yet to learn these more advanced study strategies. Never fear! *Anyone* can learn these strategies, and taking the time to do so will set you on a path to becoming a self-sufficient, independent learner.

## Understanding How You Learn

In Chapter 1, you developed a time management and study plan, which you then reassessed and redeveloped for midterm preparation in Chapter 3. In Chapter 2, you learned how to activate your brain for learning, and you identified your learning style preferences. Having taken those important steps toward understanding and planning your learning, it is time to build on that basic foundation with proven study skills and a deeper understanding of how learning happens.

The word for this kind of understanding is *metacognition*. The base word "cognition" comes from the Latin *cognitio*(-) "to get to know." In English, cognition refers to the process of acquiring knowledge through thought, through experience and the five senses, and through study. The prefix "meta" comes from the Greek μετα which means "with, around, or beyond" and in English has come to be self-referential or to mean "about the thing in question." The English word metacognition, then, refers to knowing about knowing, or thinking about thinking, or thinking about understanding. *The term metacognition refers to the way you as a student understand how you learn, or how you think about your own learning process.*

Building on that definition, metacognition is also about understanding how you absorb and process information so that you can better hone your learning skills. Your ability to learn is essential to your success in college, but that is only a first step. Learning will be equally important as you learn the skills for a career, learn how to navigate your life as you reach new milestones, and set new goals. The better you understand your learning process, the better you will be able to learn.

## Figure 5.1:   The Learning Process.

### The Learning Process

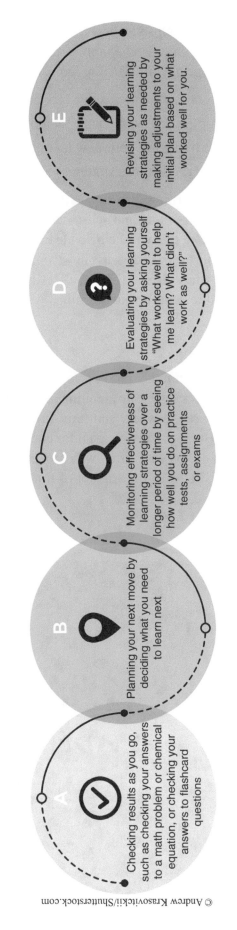

A — Checking results as you go, such as checking your answers to a math problem or chemical equation, or checking your answers to flashcard questions

B — Planning your next move by deciding what you need to learn next

C — Monitoring effectiveness of learning strategies over a longer period of time by seeing how well you do on practice tests, assignments or exams

D — Evaluating your learning strategies by asking yourself "What worked well to help me learn? What didn't work as well?"

E — Revising your learning strategies as needed by making adjustments to your initial plan based on what worked well for you.

Understanding your learning helps you become a more independent student. The more you understand about your learning process, the more you are able to control and direct your learning. Here's what being in charge of your learning looks like:

1.  You check whether your learning process is giving you the desired results.
2.  You plan your next move (stay with what is working, change what is not working)
3.  You monitor the effectiveness of your new learning strategies.
4.  Then, you evaluate and revise those strategies as needed.

Being in control of your learning also means that you will develop more mature habits including goal setting, self-observation, and self-assessment. Notice that the process described is not about finding the *one thing* that will help you learn better. It is instead about being aware, courageous, and flexible – able to see and assess how your learning is going, courageous enough to stay with your goals even when discouraged, and flexible enough to try new strategies and to change your habits as needed to benefit your learning.

## Planning and Goal Setting

By now you are no stranger to planning your time and your study in general. This chapter is your opportunity to dig deeper and consider how planning and goal setting can help you achieve your academic goals day-to-day, week-to-week, and term-to-term. Have you ever heard the saying "work smarter not harder"? Having a specific goal for each study session will help you make the most effective and efficient use of your time, which over the term can mean better academic success plus a better balance between the amount of time you need to study, and the time you can spend doing other things.

© seanbear/Shutterstock.com

You learned in Chapter 2 about setting SMART goals. You can take those SMART goals to the next level by applying your knowledge about your courses and materials to make your goals even more specific, measurable, achievable, relevant, and time-bound (SMART), and by placing those goals within a framework that helps you keep an eye on what you aim to achieve while making adjustments along the way to determine how you will get there.

**Content and Process Goals** One way to reframe your goals is to consider the differences between content and process goals. A content goal involves the knowledge that you wish to learn, whereas a process goal involves how you will go about learning that knowledge.

For example, you might set a goal to spend the next 2 hours reading chapter 5 of your Anatomy textbook. This is a content goal. It addresses the *what*, the material or content that you want to cover (chapter 5 of your Anatomy text). The next thing to consider is *how* you will go about learning the material in chapter 5. Will you read and learn by underlining, outlining, taking notes, creating flashcards, testing yourself, or some combination of those? Let's imagine that you have decided that you will spend the first hour reading through the chapter, underlining important points and making notes of important vocabulary terms and definitions. In the second hour, you have decided to see how you are doing with the material so far, and either continue the process (if it is working for you and you aren't finished with the chapter yet), or change your strategy. If underlining really isn't helping you learn the material, you might choose to shift to creating an annotated outline of the chapter, or create flashcards to test yourself on important terms and concepts. At the end of the study session, you would assess again to determine what **content** your next study session will include, and what **process** is most effective for you in learning this particular material.

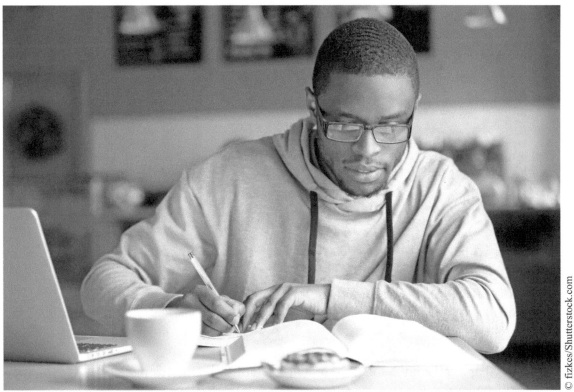

In the example above, the study plan is not only SMART, but it also includes content *and* process goals. The plan also includes flexible and intelligent engagement with the learning process, by monitoring the effectiveness of your study as you go along, and revising your plan as needed. The beauty of a process goal is that it is completely individual and personalized – it is about discovering what works best for *you*. Every student in your class might have the same content goal (to learn the material in the chapter assigned, for instance), but you and your fellow students will choose a wide variety of ways to accomplish that learning. Your goal as a student is to discover and use the ways in which you learn best, and to make that learning personal to you. The following sections on note-taking, active listening, and reading, will teach you a number of learning strategies you can use to further inform your process goals.

---

### Discovery

1. Think about a reading or other assignment you have coming up this week for one of your classes. How would you define the content (what) goal for that assignment? How would you define your own process (how) goal for that assignment?

   _____

   _____

   _____

---

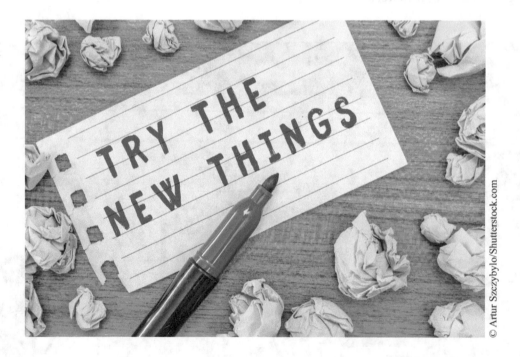

© Artur Szczybylo/Shutterstock.com

## Note-Taking Strategies

We talked in Chapters 1 and 2 about the importance of taking notes in class. When you take notes, you are creating a memory aid to help you recall what was presented in lecture. You are also creating the materials you will use to learn the material deeply, study for tests, and prepare for assignments and projects. In addition, taking notes helps you pay attention and stay focused during class so that you don't miss important concepts and information.

> *While these note taking strategies are presented in terms of capturing ideas and information from class lecture, they also work for studying your textbook and other assigned readings, and watching videos! Try these strategies as you read or watch, as another way to build your knowledge and your study materials.*

In this chapter, you will learn a variety of note-taking methods to ensure your notes are useful, purposeful, and up to the task of helping you study and learn. The note-taking methods we will cover here are the outline method, the Cornell notes method, the visual notes method, the lecture transcription method and the annotated slides method. We recommend that you try more than one and then decide which ones best fit you and the subjects you are studying. You may find that one method or the other works better in particular types of classes or learning situations, as discussed previously. When you expand your skills by learning several possible approaches, you can more easily customize your learning to what gets the best results for you.

**Outline Method** When you use the outline method, you organize what you are hearing as a series of main ideas with related or supporting information. The outline organizes the information in a structured and logical manner, creating a skeleton of the lecture subject (or textbook chapter, if you are taking notes on assigned readings). This outline serves as a study guide when you prepare for tests.

**How to use the Outline method:**

Write points in an organized manner based on space indentation:

- Place major points or main ideas farthest to the left
  - Indent secondary information under the main ideas
    - Continue indenting supplementary and supporting information under secondary information (etc.)

The advantage of the outline method is that it emphasizes the structure of ideas and the relationships between ideas. The possible disadvantage is that in a lecture that moves too quickly, it may be difficult to distinguish main ideas from supporting ideas on the fly.

Example:

I. Main Idea #1
   a. Explanation related to main idea
   b. Keywords and details related to main idea
      i. Definitions of keywords
      ii. Further information on details
   c. Examples of main idea
      i. Keywords and details related to example
II. Main Idea #2
(etc.)

## Figure 5.2:    Cornell Notetaking Method.

Name: _____          Date: _____

Class: _____          Topic: _____

| CUES | NOTES |
|---|---|
| *Written soon after class.* | *Taken during class.* |
| | – Main points |
| | – Bullet points (details, explanations) under main points |
| Anticipated exam questions | – Diagrams, charts and drawings |
| | – Paraphrase lecture |
| | – Outline |
| Main ideas, people, keywords | |
| | *Good idea to leave space between topics |
| Vocabulary | |
| | |
| Use for review and study | |

**SUMMARY**

*Written within 24 hours after class.*
Read your notes and cues above, then create a brief summary that highlights the main points in the notes on this page. Use this to find information later on as you review for assignments and tests.

*Source*: Jennifer L. Roth-Burnette, Ph.D.

*Try this method by using the template at the end of this chapter. Feel free to make copies of the template as needed.*

**Cornell Notes Method** The Cornell notes method is a note-taking strategy developed by Education professor Walter Pauk at Cornell University. Cornell notes is a structured note-taking method (like the outline method) but is also a staged method, with steps to accomplish during and after class. With Cornell notes, you divide your paper into two columns. During class, you take notes in the right column. These notes can include main points, bulleted details and explanations, drawings or diagrams, your paraphrase of the lecture, and/or an outline of the lecture, reading or videos. As soon as class is over, you place study cues from your lecture notes in the left column. These include anticipated exam questions, vocabulary terms, and important people, places, concepts and keywords. Within 24 hours after class, read over your Cornell notes pages again, and write summaries in the space at the bottom of the page. Your summaries will highlight the main points from your notes, will help cement them in your memory, and will be useful later for finding information in your notes as you prepare for assignments and tests.

**Visual Notetaking** Visual notetaking, which includes sketchnoting and mind-mapping, is considered "purposeful drawing." It is a creative way to take notes using images, lines, shapes, and doodles using paper and pen or using a tablet with stylus or digital pencil. Sketching or mapping allows you to augment your handwritten notes by reinforcing major concepts and showing relationships between ideas.

Sketchnoting, illustrated here, is a type of customized notetaking that incorporates words and phrases with sketches, drawings and other visual signs to help you learn and remember material, and to better capture the relationships between ideas. A quick internet search of "sketchnoting examples" will turn up many more examples to ignite your imagination!

**Figure 5.3: Sketchnoting.**

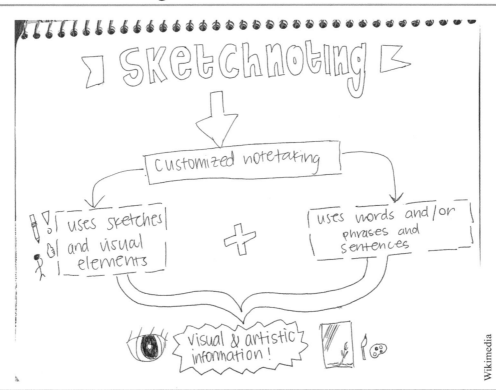

Wikimedia

**Figure 5.4:    Mind Mapping.**

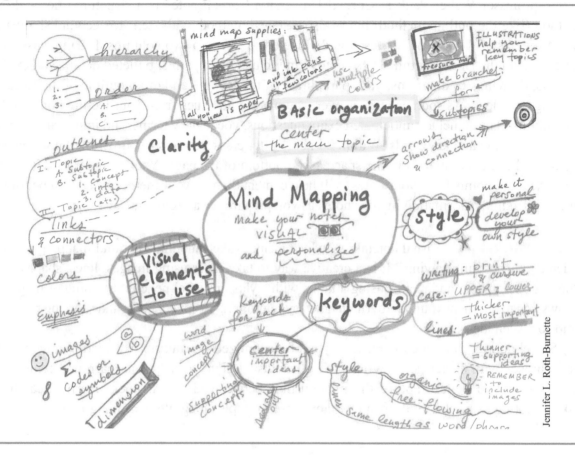

Mind-mapping is a way of diagramming thoughts and concepts visually without having to worry as much about order and structure. Mind maps can use images, keywords, shapes, colors and lines that are drawn as branches coming from one central idea or from a series of ideas. Like sketchnoting, mind-mapping is nonlinear, and captures the relationships between ideas.

**Lecture Transcription**  If you have a fast and accurate typing speed, you could try lecture transcription. In a study conducted at Washington University in St. Louis, students who were assigned to transcribe a lecture using a computer (meaning they attempted to type everything their professor said during the lecture into a document on their computer) fared better on immediate recall than their peers who had used an organized note-taking method (like Cornell notes) or who had tried to transcribe the lecture by hand. Later, the students who had used an organized method (like outline or Cornell notes) did better on longer-term recall. However, once all students were allowed to review and study their notes, the group who transcribed the lecture fared better in longer-term recall. Your takeaway from this? If lecture transcription is your preferred option, remember that reviewing your notes later is also essential to the learning process.

**Annotated Slides**  If you are in a class in which your professor lectures using a power point or similar presentation method, and makes those lecture slides available to you prior to lecture, you can use those slides as a starting point for your notes. Download the slides ahead of time and save them in a format where you can add notes to them on your computer or tablet, or print them so that you can make notes by hand. During lecture, use the outline method or the lecture transcription method to annotate (add notes to) your slides. Your annotated slides then become your study materials for future review, assignments, projects and tests.

> *Food for Thought: Students in a nationwide sample of learners participated in a note-taking experiment. Those who attended power point lectures reported that when they did not have the slides ahead of time, they took notes on what was on the slides. However, students who had the slides ahead of time primarily took notes on what the professor said about the slides. Which group had better notes?*

**Taking it up a Notch** Now that you have some ideas about how to approach note taking, use these strategies to make the most of your notes:

- **Cultivate active listening**. You will take better notes if you are a critical and discriminating listener. Just as in the active reading described in Chapter 2, active listening means that you are thinking and asking questions along with the speaker. As you go along, make notes of your questions or ideas that you need clarification on. After lecture, bring those questions to your study group, see whether your assigned reading answers some of those questions, or email your professor about your questions. Your persistence will pay off with better knowledge of the material. The next segment of this chapter will offer a deeper understanding of active listening.

- **Write your notes by hand** if possible (unless you are attempting the lecture transcription method above). Research on learning has demonstrated that students remember their notes better and do better on quizzes and tests based on those notes, when they took notes by hand. The reasons for this have to do with the brain's connection to the kinetic activity of writing – actually having to form the letters – which makes it more memorable to your brain than typing words by a series of keystrokes.

- **Review your notes within 24 hours** and again within 72 hours. Taking notes is only part of the equation! Reviewing them cements them more firmly in your memory and helps you later with improved recall of the subject matter.

- **Create questions from your notes** as you review them in the first 24 hours. Then, try to answer those questions without looking directly at your notes. When you practice this several times per week, you will find that you already know more of the material when it comes time to study for major tests.

- **Create flashcards from your notes** as you review them during the first 24 hours. You can make flashcards with a set of 3" × 5" notecards, writing a question on one side, and an answer on the other. The activity of making the flashcards, writing both the questions and the answers, will place the material more firmly in your memory. Testing yourself with the flashcards (asking yourself a question, and trying your best to answer it correctly before checking yourself with the answer on the back) will further help you memorize material. Flashcards work especially well for scientific vocabulary and concepts, foreign language vocabulary, history facts and dates, and any other subject matter than contains words, dates, facts, definitions, and discrete concepts you need to remember.

## Active Listening

Active listening is a vital communication skill that will help you succeed in college as well as in your career. Research shows that students who practice active listening have higher levels of academic success than students who do not. Research also shows that the ability to engage and effectively communicate with your team members on the job is essential to your performance in many career sectors. Active listening is something you can go ahead and begin developing right now, in college!

Active listening is not just hearing. For example, if you put in your ear pods and play some music with a good beat to energize you during a workout, you are more likely engaging in passive hearing. The music is part of your auditory environment but you may not be particularly focused on it. It remains closer to the background of your awareness, like the soundtrack of a movie. Active listening, on the other hand, means that you are actively focused on the speaker (in the case of a lecture or a conversation), and you are doing active mental work to understand and process all that is being said. With active listening, the goal is to understand the speaker so well that you would be able to paraphrase, or accurately say back to them what you heard them say.

Active listening is not a skill people are born with – it needs to be learned and practiced. One of the keys to growing your active listening skill is paying attention to when you struggle to listen actively due to the situation or even due to personal bias. Just as you are learning to practice empathy toward yourself, practicing an empathetic mindset in the classroom – toward your classmates, graduate assistants, faculty and others – will help you better understand their point of view, and what they are saying.

---

**DISCOVERY**

1.  Think of your auditory experiences (experiences of hearing and listening) over the past 24 hours. Identify times when you were passively hearing things in your environment. Identify one or two times in which you were actively listening. (If you aren't sure, a clue to active listening is that you remember and can still repeat or paraphrase what was said.)

    _____

    _____

    _____

2.  How much effort did each of those auditory experiences require of you? How well do you remember each of those auditory experiences?

    _____

    _____

    _____

Active listening can also inform and assist your note-taking. Watching the speaker carefully for nonverbal cues and body language can help you understand which points in a lecture may be more important than others. Practicing *paraphrasing* what you are hearing is a way to ensure you are focused and listening with attention, and also gives you some of the material you can write in your notes. Asking questions, even to yourself, about what you are hearing helps you think critically about the material, understand it better, and know what you need to follow up on later if your questions remain at the end of lecture. In a classroom discussion setting, active listening can help you contribute with greater confidence, as your responses will be shaped by a clearer understanding of the question and of the perspectives of your classmates.

© Sarawut Aiemsinsuk/Shutterstock.com

Complete the following exercise to practice your active listening skills. Start by identifying a subject for your active listening. This could be a recorded lecture or an assigned video for one of your classes, a guest speaker at a club or organization, or you could ask a friend or a family member to tell you a story. During your active listening practice, take these steps, adapted from Heather Syrett's Active Listening in the Classroom:

1. **Focus on what is being said**. Give the speaker you undivided attention. Clear your mind of everything else.

2. **Do not prejudge or assume you already know** the material. Your goal is to understand what the person is saying; you don't need to agree with it.

3. **Repeat what you just heard**. (This is the paraphrasing mentioned in the paragraphs above.) If you are having a one-on-one conversation, confirm with the speaker that what you heard is what they said. If you listened to a recorded lecture or video, review the material to make sure you heard what was said. If you attended a live presentation, check with another attendee to see if you heard what they heard.

4. Ask the speaker to **expand or clarify** what they just said to you (in a one-on-one conversation) or listen for expanding and clarifying remarks (in a lecture situation).

5. If you are unsure about what the speaker is saying, **ask questions**, or make note of questions to ask later. Do not assume you know or understand.

6. As you listen to the speaker (whether one-on-one, recorded, or in a live speaker setting)**, listen for verbal cues and watch for nonverbal cues**. Verbal cues include statements like "this is an important point" or "I want to make sure everyone understand this concept." Nonverbal cues include facial expressions, body positioning, arm and hand gestures, and tone of voice. For example, the speaker might repeat himself, get louder, or start using more hand gestures.

7. **Listen for requests**. A speaker may ask questions designed to engage you more deeply in the material they present, or may ask members of the class to raise their hands in response to a question. These are *direct* requests. A speaker may also hide a request as a statement of a problem. For example, if a friend says "I hate math!" they might mean "Can you help me figure out a solution to this problem?" This is an *indirect* request.

Once you have completed the above active listening practice activity you can reflect on how you did by answering the Discovery questions below

---

### DISCOVERY

1. How effectively were you able to focus on the speaker, and for how long?

   _____

   _____

   _____

2. How successful was your attempt to paraphrase the speaker? What did you paraphrase correctly? What did you miss?

   _____

   _____

   _____

3. What kinds of questions did you ask or note down?

   _____

   _____

   _____

4. What verbal and nonverbal cues did you notice?

   _____

   _____

   _____

5. Did you pick up on any direct or indirect requests? What were they?

   _____

   _____

   _____

---

Don't do this just once! Take opportunities every day to practice and hone your active listening, whether in class, with your friends, at organizational meetings, or elsewhere. Use the guiding questions above to continue improving your active listening skills.

## Reading at the College Level

If there is one thing many students say they find difficult about college, it's the reading. Typically, college classes have much more assigned reading than students have experienced previously, and often it is at a more challenging level than they have had to face before. Many of the strategies for notetaking also work well for reading. The outline method and the Cornell notes method of notetaking in particular work exceptionally well for organizing what you are reading and creating the study materials that will help you remember what you have read. These methods also offer an easy way to get back to the right spot in your textbook or assigned reading for any further questions, clarification or review.

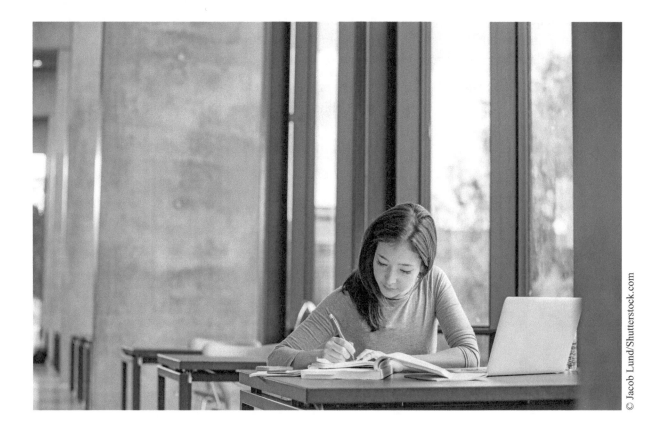

© Jacob Lund/Shutterstock.com

This section will offer an additional, in-depth reading strategy commonly called SQ3R. SQ3R is an acronym that stands for Survey, Question, Read, Recite, and Review. These five steps were proposed by Francis Robinson in the mid-20th century and continue to be viewed as a highly effective strategy for comprehending and learning what you read. Following these steps will help you engage *intentionally* with your reading and increase your understanding of the text.

**Survey (S)**: The survey step gives you a framework for understanding the basics of what you are about to read. Begin by skimming over or paging through the assigned text in order to gain an initial understanding of it. Read headings and summaries. As you survey, ask yourself these questions:

- How long is it, or how many pages?
- What headings and subheadings do I see?
- What charts or illustrations do I see?
- What is this text about?

**Question (Q):** The question step activates your mind for learning. Now that you have surveyed the text, formulate questions. These could be general, such as "What do I expect to learn from this text?" or "How will this text benefit my learning in this class?" You might also try converting each heading or subheading into a question such as "What is ____?" or "What will I learn about ____?" Write your questions down. You'll need them later!

**Read (R1):** Now that you have laid a foundation of knowledge about the structure of the text, and formulated some questions about it, you are prepared for *active* reading. Your awareness of the structure and your questions help you to focus as you read through the text. Try to keep moving through it, even if there is something difficult that you do not understand. (You will be able to come back to difficult sections later.)

**Recite (R2), also called Recall:** Look back at the questions you wrote down earlier. In your own words, try to answer these questions, either by speaking them out loud or by writing the answers. This step helps you internalize and conceptualize what you are learning. Were any of your questions easy to answer? Were any of your questions difficult to answer?

## Figure 5.5:   SQ3R Reading Strategy.

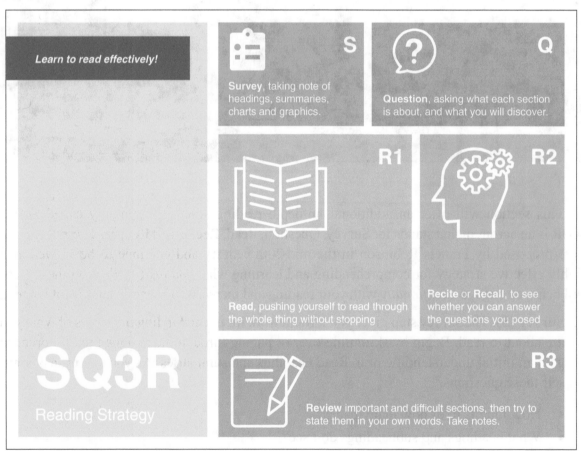

*Source: Jennifer Roth-Burnette, Ph.D.*

**Review (R3):** Go back and read important or difficult sections again slowly. Remember why you are reading to keep your mind active. Take notes as you review so that you can remember important information and where you read it.

## Test Preparation

If you have maintained the basic success habits outlined in Chapter 1 (reading assigned materials before class, taking notes during class, reviewing after class) you will have done a great deal of test preparation before you "officially" begin studying for your tests. In addition, many students say that they benefit from extra test preparation starting 5 to 7 days ahead of a test, with an additional 1 to 2 hours of study and review each day. Use the following lists of "dos" and avoid the "do nots" for best college test preparation:

### <u>DO</u>

1. **Study Ahead.** Set aside 1 to 2 extra study hours each day for 5 to 7 days ahead of your test in a given class. Use that time to review your notes and readings and try to restate the main ideas and concepts in your own words. If it is a problem-based class like Math or Accounting, use the extra study time to review and practice solving problems.

2. **Participate in Academic Supports.** Attend tutoring and test review sessions offered by your college, or the graduate assistant or professor for your class.

3. **Complete a Practice Test.** Many textbooks include practice test questions, or your professor might make those available to you. Give yourself a time limit to see how many questions you can answer correctly without referring to your notes or your textbook. Then, you will know what areas you need to focus on more as you prepare for the actual test.

4. **Find a Study Group.** Studying together with other students enrolled in your class is an ideal way to review together, compare notes, explain ideas to one another, and quiz one another. Set an agenda and a time frame for each group study session.

5. **Keep Your Ears Open.** Many professors will tell you during lectures when a particular idea is going to be on an upcoming test or exam.

6. **Get Plenty of Sleep.** A rested brain and body are a capable brain and body! Students who get a good night's sleep right before a test or exam do better on that test or exam.

### <u>DO NOT</u>

1. **Cram at the Last Minute.** Staying up all night right before a test or exam can leave your brain and body exhausted, reducing your ability to think and remember information. It's much better for brain, body and memory to prepare gradually over several days.

2. **Multi-task While Studying.** Trying to study while distracted by messages, social media, and videos makes it much more difficult for your brain to absorb the information you are trying to learn. Set aside time to study without distractions, and then reward yourself with some media or phone time after your study session is done.

3.   **Let Outside Influences Change Your Plans.** If you have planned to study for a test, stick to your plans. Try to keep your relationships with family, friends, and significant others drama-free and ask them to understand your need to focus on test preparation for a few days. Once the test is done, plan to do something fun together.

**Different Types of Tests**   A major component of preparing for college tests is knowing in advance what the test will be like. The advice above on taking practice tests will help with this, but in addition, look through your syllabus, listen carefully to your professor in class, and if you still have questions ask them directly:

- What will the test cover?
- What kind of test will it be? (Multiple choice, essay, true–false, problem solving?)
- How much time is allotted for the test?
- How will students answer the test? (Blue book, computer, answer sheet?)
- Are there penalties for guessing?
- Does every question on the test have equal value?
- How will the test be graded?
- Do I need any special supplies?

Knowing these basic facts about your test will help you better prepare. Read on for tips on how to prepare for a variety of test types.

## Multiple Choice: Choosing Answers

Multiple choice questions have two components: an incomplete statement or question known as a **stem**, and a series of possible answers or **options**. Usually, the instructions will tell you to select the answer that is the best option. Your job is to find the answer that is the *best*, or the *most* correct, not just any reasonable-seeming good answer.

Students run into problems when they do not read the stem (the question) carefully enough, or do not fully understand it. If you are not sure you understand what the stem is asking, reread it before looking at the options. You might even want to cross out the answers that you know are incorrect, so that you can focus on selecting the best answer from the remaining options.

## Matching Tests: Factual Knowledge

Matching tests typically have two columns of information. Students must match each entry in one column to the correct response in the other column. You may occasionally take a matching test with more than two columns.

Read the instructions of a matching test carefully, and pay attention to whether some of the answers might be used more than once. If answers cannot be used more than once, cross them out as you use them. If you cannot match a particular item, skip it and then come back to it when you have more of the other matches complete. It will be easier to determine the answer from the remaining choices.

## True–False: Two Choices

True-false tests give you a choice of two answers in which only one is the correct response. Prepare for these much as you would for multiple choice tests, as they also test your knowledge of facts.

After reading a statement, decide whether it is true or false. Many students make the mistake of reading too quickly and not fully understanding a statement, and risk misunderstanding it. Read slowly and carefully, be sure you fully understand the statement, and then decide whether the statement is true or false. Pay attention to words like *always, all, never,* and *none,* which may indicate a false statement.

## Completion: Blanks You Fill In

In completion tests, students must supply a correct word, phrase, number, date, symbol, or complete a statement. You may be given a word bank with correct answers to help you out. Prepare for this test in the same way you would any test based on factual knowledge. In particular, pay attention to vocabulary and keywords.

## Essay Questions: Organize Ahead

Essay tests are often daunting to students, but they don't have to be as scary as they seem. Essay tests usually focus the main points or concepts that have been discussed in your class and/or your assigned readings. You will need to know facts and details related to these main points. Unlike the other test types mentioned in this section, essay tests require you to remember information to write an answer, rather than select it from given material. The best way to prepare for an essay test is to practice speaking and writing answers to questions you have made up during your study process, questions the professor mentioned in class, or questions at the end of a textbook chapter.

You will do best on an essay test if you take a moment to organize your thoughts before you begin writing. Some students note down a quick outline of their answer before they begin writing a long essay. If you run into a question for which you are not sure of the answer, go ahead and at least attempt a partial answer for partial credit (rather than give no answer for no credit). Often, just starting to write an answer will help the answer come to you, or help you remember additional details you should include.

## Chapter Summary

This is a chapter you can return to again and again for tips and reminders about various ways to take notes, listen actively, read and learn effectively, and prepare for tests. The most important point about these studies and learning strategies is to identify the ones that work best for you and for the subjects you are studying, and to make adjustments as necessary. Having the courage and flexibility to evaluate your own progress, and to grow and make changes as needed, will help you be successful both in college and in your broader life.

## End-of-Chapter Activities

I. **Grit Revisit.** It's not unusual to feel your focus drift a little through the course of the academic term. If you have lost a little of your initial enthusiasm or focus, this is a good time to return to the ideas of grit and growth mindset. Answer the following questions:

1. What are my goals for the rest of this academic term?

   _____

   _____

   _____

2. What are my goals for this academic year?

   _____

   _____

   _____

3. What am I trying to accomplish by attending college?

   _____

   _____

   _____

4. What am I learning about myself?

   _____

   _____

   _____

*Pro tip: Keep yourself inspired! Write your answers to these questions on a post-it and place them on your mirror or your refrigerator where you will see them on a daily basis.*

II. **Try a New Note-Taking Method.** Select two (or more) different note-taking methods to try, and try one for each of the next two or three class meetings. Tear-out Templates for Cornell Notes are provided on the following pages. After you try two or more, answer the questions below:

1. Which works best for you in the classroom?

   _____

   _____

   _____

2. Which results in notes that are easiest for you to review and study afterward?

   _____

   _____

   _____

Name: _____     Date: _____

Class: _____     Topic: _____

| CUES | NOTES |
|------|-------|
|      |       |

**SUMMARY**

Name: _____    Date: _____

Class: _____    Topic: _____

| CUES | NOTES |
|------|-------|
|      |       |

**SUMMARY**

Name: _____     Date: _____

Class: _____     Topic: _____

| CUES | NOTES |
|---|---|
| | |

**SUMMARY**

Name: _____  Date: _____

Class: _____  Topic: _____

| CUES | NOTES |
|------|-------|
|      |       |

**SUMMARY**

**III. Test Preparation Checklist.** Use the following test-preparation checklist to gain the information you need on upcoming tests. Remember to look for answers in the syllabus first, and in any course information provided by the professor (on the online course site, for instance). If you cannot identify all of the answers there, reach out to your graduate assistant or professor for additional information.

1. What will the test cover?

   _____

   _____

   _____

2. What kind of test will it be? (Multiple choice, essay, true-false, problem solving?)

   _____

   _____

   _____

3. How much time is allotted for the test?

   _____

   _____

   _____

4. How will students answer the test? (Blue book, computer, answer sheet?)

   _____

5. Are there penalties for guessing?

   _____

   _____

   _____

6. Does every question on the test have equal value?

   _____

   _____

   _____

7. How will the test be graded?

   _____

   _____

   _____

8. Do I need any special supplies?

   _____

   _____

   _____

# References

Barbouta, A., Barbouta, C., & Kotrotsiou, S. (2020). Growth mindset and grit: How do university students' mindsets and grit affect their academic achievement? *International Journal of Caring Sciences, 13*(1), 654-664.

Boley, D. A. (2008). Use of premade mind maps to enhance simulation learning. *Nurse Educator, 33*(5), 220-223.

Bui, D. C., Myerson, J., & Hale, S. (2013). Note-taking with computers: Exploring alternative strategies for improved recall. *Journal of Educational Psychology, 105*(2), 299-309. https://doi.org/10.1037/a0030367

Crumb, R. M., Hildebrandt, R., & Sutton, T. M. (2020). The value of handwritten notes: A failure to find state-dependent effects when using a laptop to take notes and complete a quiz. *Teaching of Psychology*, 1. https://doi.org/10.1177/0098628320979895

Dweck, C. S. (2006). *Mindset: The new psychology of success*. Random House.

Eberts, M., & Gisler, M. (1998). *Prepare for college*. NTC Contemporary.

Edwards-Groves, C., & Davidson, C. (2020). Noticing the multidimensionality of active listening in a dialogic classroom. *Australian Journal of Language & Literacy, 43*(1), 83-94.

Flippo, R. F., & Caverly, D. C. (2000). *Handbook of college reading and study strategy research*. Taylor and Francis Ltd.

Hensley, L. C. (2020). Assessing academic strategies in college learning centers: Considerations for scholarly practitioners. *Learning Assistance Review (TLAR), 25*(1), 81-101.

Kiewra, K. A., Mayer, R. E., Christensen, M., Kim, S.-I., & Risch, N. (1991). Effects of repetition on recall and note-taking: Strategies for learning from lectures. *Journal of Educational Psychology, 83*(1), 120-123. https://doi.org/10.1037/0022-0663.83.1.120

Laurie, R. (2003). *Test taking strategies & study skills for the utterly confused*. McGraw-Hill Education.

Marbella International University Centre. (2020). *What is the SQ3R study method and how to use it?* https://miuc.org/sq3r-study-method/

Paulson, E. J., & Bauer, L. (2011). Goal setting as an explicit element of metacognitive reading and study strategies for college reading. *NADE Digest, 5*(3), 41-49.

Robinson, C. (2018, 02/2018). Note-taking strategies in the science classroom [Article]. *Science Scope, 41*(6), 22-25. https://doi.org/10.2505/4/ss18_041_06_22

Robinson, F. P. (1946). *Effective study*. Harper & Brothers.

Syrett, H. (2021). *Active listening in the classroom*. Austin Community College. https://courses.lumenlearning.com/austincc-learningframeworks/chapter/chapter-10-active-listening-in-the-classroom/

Wong, L. (2015). *Essential study skills*. Cengage Learning.

Yeager, D., & Dweck, C. (2012). Mindsets that promote resilience: When students believe that personal characteristics can be developed. *Educational Psychologist, 47*(4), 302-314. https://doi.org/10.1080/00461520.2012.722805

Yeager, D. S., & Dweck, C. S. (2020). What can be learned from growth mindset controversies? *American Psychologist, 75*(9), 1269-1284. https://doi.org/10.1037/amp0000794

Zhao, H., Xiong, J., Zhang, Z., & Qi, C. (2021). Growth mindset and college students' learning engagement during the COVID-19 pandemic: A serial mediation model. *Frontiers in Psychology.* https://doi.org/10.3389/fpsyg.2021.621094

## Chapter 6

# Mindfulness

| Choices of Successful Students | Choices of Struggling Students |
|---|---|
| 1. Do not allow negative emotions or thoughts fester, and intentionally work to find the positive in each situation, or just let negativity go. | 1. Let negative emotions or thoughts remain in their minds, allowing them to negatively affect their physical and mental wellness, and college success. |
| 2. Intentionally seek to identify triggers that cause strong emotions, and manage them effectively as they come. | 2. Float through life allowing strong emotions to impact them negatively almost daily. |
| 3. Allow their strong emotions to pass before making important decisions. | 3. Make important decisions while experiencing strong emotions, often regretting the decision later. |
| 4. Show empathy for others' emotions and are intentional in responding positively to others' strong emotions, resulting in better and more meaningful relationships. | 4. Are unaware on others' emotions and how their own emotions and actions affect others. |
| 5. Learn their own cognitive distortions and intentionally try to be positive thinkers. | 5. Allow negative thinking to be a burden on their emotional and physical wellness. |
| 6. Seamlessly adjust to barriers that may otherwise delay or disrupt their achieving of their goals. | 6. Panic or give up when barriers outside of their control disrupt or delay their ability to achieve their goals. |
| 7. Are able to say "no" when saying "yes" may disrupt their ability to achieve their goals. | 7. Are unable to say "no" to family or friends who may be pushing them off their path toward achieving their goals. |
| 8. Learn how to effectively manage anxiety or stress. | 8. Allow stress and anxiety to control their lives. |
| 9. Show resilience and are hopeful. | 9. Give up easily and do not see the future in a positive light. |

## Introduction

Your college success depends heavily on how well you do in classes. How well you do in classes, as you have already learned, depends on your willingness and motivation to learn, how you network and utilize resources, how you engage with your college and university, and how you cultivate academic skills. As you are about to find out, your emotions and thought processes can also have a significant impact on your college success and happiness in general. In this chapter, you will learn key concepts for developing *Mindfulness*, or the ability to live in the moment as opposed to dwelling on the past or anticipating the future.

Rooted in Buddhism and Hinduism, and popularized in Western cultures in the late 1970s, mindfulness is composed of 2 concepts: awareness and acceptance. *Awareness* helps you focus on your inner emotions and thoughts in the present moment, while *acceptance* is the ability to come to terms with your emotions and thoughts, rather than judge or avoid them. Mindfulness can help you avoid self-criticism or doubt and thus a great tool for finding inner-peace, as well as for improving your relationships with others.

### Focus Questions:

1. What is emotional intelligence, and why is it so important?
2. How do your emotions affect your learning?
3. What are some ways you can harness your thoughts for building college and life success?

© Maurizio Milanesio/Shutterstock.com

# Letting Go

As human beings with human brains we all exhibit and experience a wide and complex range of emotions and thoughts. Our emotions and thoughts play a major role in who we are, how we behave, how we interact with others, and how others perceive us. Positive emotions and thoughts make us feel good and help us find joy in our lives. Negative emotions and thoughts, however, can be a tremendous burden, not only preventing us from finding joy in our lives, but also affecting the choices we make and how we live our lives in general. Learning how to identify and manage both positive and negative emotions is an important skill for leading successful and joyous lives.

If you have ever traveled somewhere on a long trip where you had to bring a lot of luggage, you are probably familiar with how too much luggage can be burdensome. If you travel by automobile, too much luggage can weigh you down and take up space that might otherwise be useful for a more comfortable journey. If traveling by plane or train with a lot of luggage, you have to haul it in to the station or airport, wait in line to check it, stop and pick it up when you arrive to your destination, then load it back into a vehicle. On top of all of that, you may be paying additional "baggage fees" to bring this burdensome luggage with you.

This "baggage fees" concept of paying extra for potentially unnecessary and burdensome luggage can also apply to your "emotional baggage." Carrying too many, or unnecessary negative emotions or thoughts can be disruptive to a comfortable journey through your college experience. Carrying emotional baggage, or unresolved emotions can bring a "fee" of their own that is not monetary, but is instead the cost of disruption to your life, and the risk that being weighed down by emotional baggage will prevent you from achieving your goals. Learning emotional intelligence and how your thinking can affect your emotions can be beneficial for reducing this baggage.

---

### DISCOVERY

Consider the following mind map representing positive and negative emotions. Take 2 to 3 deep breaths and then weigh each emotion listed on the map. Which emotions do you experience on a daily basis? Which do you experience at least once per week?

1. Circle or color in the emotions that you feel on a regular basis.

2. Are there emotions you feel frequently that are not listed here? If so, add them, drawing lines to connect them to the positive or negative centers.

3. Now, without judging yourself harshly, describe your personal balance between positive and negative emotions.

_____

_____

_____

You have just taken a solid step toward exercising your emotional intelligence by engaging your **awareness.**

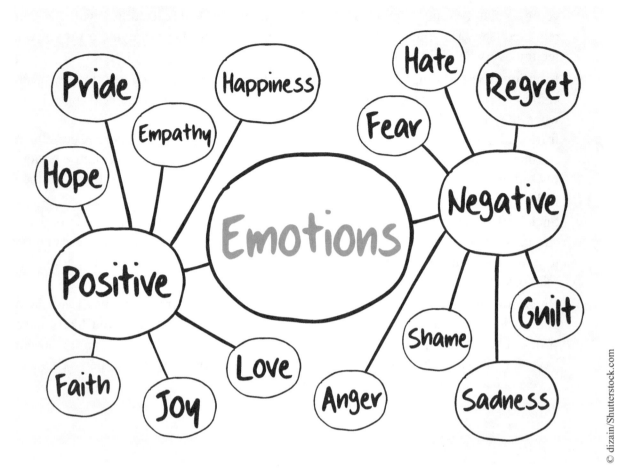

© dizain/Shutterstock.com

## Emotional Intelligence

You have probably heard of the intelligence quotient or "IQ" whose purpose is to provide a score for an individual's ability to reason or use logic to solve problems or make predictions. A high IQ is considered beneficial for college and future success of course, but there are many other variables that influence your academic success. As you learned already in Chapter 5 on Growth Mindset, no matter your level of talent or intellectual ability, you can still learn. Your emotional intelligence also plays a large role in your college success.

Emotional intelligence refers to your ability to identify and manage your own emotions, as well as appropriately identify and respond to the emotions of others. According to *Emotional Intelligence* (2005) by Daniel Goleman, there are four primary components to emotional intelligence: emotional self-awareness, emotional self-management, social awareness, and relationship management. The first two depend on your understanding and management of *your own* emotions, while the latter two depend on your understanding and management of *others'* emotions.

- **Emotional self-awareness** is knowing your own feelings in that moment. Understanding when you are angry, upset, stressed, happy, or bored, as well as what triggers may cause them, are the first steps to managing strong emotions. Too often people do not know how to anticipate strong emotions, and as a result allow them to take control. Have you ever felt a strong emotion, and before you knew it, had reacted in a way that you regretted later? Do you ever "check-out" and put assignments or studying off if you are feeling overwhelmed?

- **Emotional Self-Management** is not learning how stop having strong emotions, instead, emotional self-management is learning how to not allow strong emotions to control you when they arrive. Especially in a new environment, you are likely to become angry, frustrated, sad, anxious, or excited at some point. Those of us who have strong emotional self-management skills *do not* make critical decisions during a time of high emotion. Instead, we allow strong emotions to pass and consider our options carefully. We then make the decision that best support our aspirations.

- **Social Awareness** refers to your ability to empathize with others' emotions. If you have strong social awareness skills, you are aware of others' emotions such as sadness or anxiety, and more likely to show compassion for them. Social awareness is important for relationship management.

- **Relationship Management** refers to how you respond to others' emotions. If you are a good listener, are cooperative, and work well with others in groups, you likely have strong relationship management skills. If, however, you are confrontational or do not have empathy for others, you probably have difficulty working with others. This can have a negative impact on your college experience.

## Figure 6.1:    Emotional Intelligence.

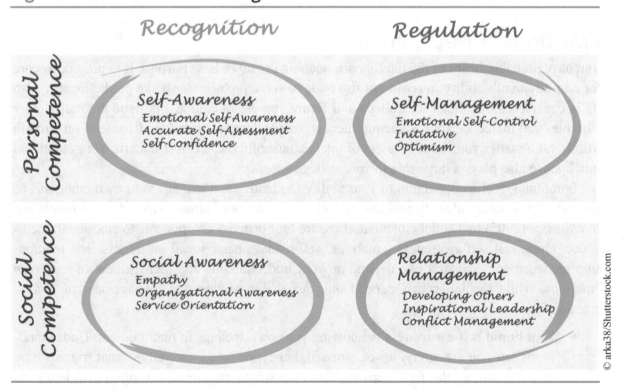

DISCOVERY

Are you aware of your emotions as they are taking place? Are you able to effectively manage them without reacting negatively? If not, how can you improve your self-awareness and self-management? Use the questions below to explore your own emotional intelligence.

1.  Write down both positive and negative strong emotions that you have felt in the last month. Identify when you have been sad, depressed, angry, frustrated, happy, excited, nervous or anxious.

    _____

    _____

    _____

2.  Now think about what you were doing, or what happened when you felt these strong emotions. Can you identify what triggered them? Try and distinguish subtleties between different emotions. Maybe you were nervous when introduced to a new group of people, but anxious when you were called on in class and asked to speak up.

    _____

    _____

    _____

3.  What was your response to those emotions, and were your responses appropriate? Are there any responses you made that would indicate weak emotional intelligence as described above?

    _____

    _____

    _____

4.  Now think about your interactions with others. Are you empathetic to the emotions of others? (Provide an example). How has this affected your relationships?

    _____

    _____

    _____

## Cognitive Distortions

Your ability to have strong emotional intelligence can be closely connected to your understanding of how you think. Most of the time we as humans are able to think rationally and respond appropriately when something doesn't go our way. However, for some of us, negative thinking has become second nature and impacts our emotions and behaviors on a regular basis.

Let's look at a common situation for a college student: a classmate who arrives late for a group assignment team meeting at the library. Sam, Diego, and Jasmine are classmates in their macroeconomics class and have been tasked with giving a presentation on supply and demand. When Jasmine and Diego meet at the library at the agreed-upon time, Sam is nowhere to be found. Even after 10 minutes of waiting, no sign of, or word from Sam. Jasmine becomes frustrated and says to Diego "I hate working in groups. Every time I have to work in a group someone doesn't show up or pull their weight. I hope Sam trips up the stairs when she finally does arrive."

While it is possible that Sam is a poor team member, it is also possible that there is a reasonable explanation for her not being to the group meeting on time. Either way, Jasmine's negative response is neither helping the group finish the assignment, nor helping the dynamic of the group. A response like Jasmine's can lead to negative feelings about Sam, the assignment, the class, and future group assignments for both Jasmine and Diego.

Jasmine's response could be a result of cognitive distortions, or thought patterns that cause us to view reality inaccurately, and often in negative ways. Cognitive distortions are habitual ways of thinking that when experienced often enough can lead to increases in anxiety, depression, and have a negative impact on relationships.

The following are common cognitive distortions:

1. **All or Nothing Thinking:** You think in extremes, things are black and white without any option for in-between. If a situation is not perfect, it's a failure. An example is getting a "C" on an exam when you were expecting an "A" and responding with dropping the class. You drop the class because you think there is no way you can achieve an "A" on future exams because you didn't this time.

2. **Over Generalization:** You see a single negative event, such as not passing a vocabulary test as a never-ending pattern of failure. You often use words such as "always" or "never" when thinking about it. A student might say something like "my professors never respond to my emails; they don't care if I pass or not!"

3. **Mental Filter:** You only see the negative side of something, no matter how small, and focus on that detail exclusively. Because you can only focus on the single, negative detail, the entire experience is made negative. An example is stumbling on just a few words during your presentation. Even though the rest of the presentation was good, your brief stumble makes the entire presentation a negative experience or feel like a failure.

4. **Discounting the Positive**: You reject positive experiences as not counting. When you do something well, you discredit it to something that wasn't good enough or something so simple that "anyone could do it." An example is being accepted in to a club or elected to a leadership position and discrediting it to "nobody else must have applied, or they'll take anyone." Discounting the positive takes the joy out of life and is a contributor and result of low confidence.

5. **Jumping to Conclusions:** You interpret things negatively when facts are missing. You may "mind read" and assume someone doesn't like you or is reacting negatively to you, or "fortune tell" and predict that the result will be bad. Examples include saying "my professor doesn't like me" without evidence, or "I'll never pass calculus class."

6. **Magnification:** You magnify or exaggerate your less desirable qualities and minimize your desirable qualities. Also known as the binocular trick, you may ignore your writing talents and instead focus on how you get nervous when public speaking.

7. **Emotional Reasoning:** You assume your negative feelings reflect reality. Examples include "I get nervous when meeting new people, I must be socially awkward," or "she doesn't seem to like me, I must not be good enough." Oftentimes these conclusions are figments of our imagination.

8. **Should Statements:** Should statements such as "I shouldn't have mixed up those dates on my history exam" can lead to guilt, frustration, and a desire to give up. Should statements directed at others such as "he should be more organized" lead to anger and frustration toward that person. Oftentimes people use should statements as motivation but inherently are assuming inadequacy which can result to negativity, anxiety, or overcompensation.

9. **Labeling:** Labeling is an extreme form of all-or-nothing thinking whereas you may label yourself as "dumb," "awkward," or otherwise inadequate. Labeling is irrational because you are not exclusively how you act or react each time. Labeling can lead to anger, anxiety, and low self-esteem.

   Labeling someone else as a "jerk" or something similar after a single interaction, without knowing the underlying reasons for their behavior, or without knowing what they may be thinking can lead to hostility toward that person and feelings of hopelessness.

10. **Personalization and Blame:** Personalization is holding yourself responsible for something negative that isn't entirely under your control. When a friend withdraws from their math course and you think "had only I tutored her, she may have been able to pass" you are personalizing something outside of your control. Personalization can lead to guilt, shame, and feelings of inadequacy.

   Blaming refers to blaming others entirely for a result that you may have contributed to as well. An example is blaming a friend for having to leave college when you may have pressured them often in to avoiding studying to go out and have fun. While their college success is ultimately their responsibility, your peer pressure may have contributed to their doing poorly in classes. This of course also applies to blaming others for your own shortcomings such as your professor for a difficult test, or your advisor for not having an appointment slot open last minute, resulting in your not being able to register on time. While blaming can protect your ego, it is damaging to relationships and is still a cognitive distortion.

Reframing cognitive distortions is not easy. Most people cannot just switch their cognitive distortions off like a light switch. These can take time and effort to change, especially if you have become accustomed to thinking in this way. Below are recommendations for reframing cognitively distorted thinking:

1. Try to identify negative beliefs, self-talk, or emotions as they are taking place. Just as in improving your emotional intelligence, the first step to change negative thinking is to identify it when it is likely to happen or when it is actually taking place.

    Example: "I'm beginning to feel nervous and sick to my stomach, and my heart rate is increasing because of this presentation I have to give."

2. Identify the cognitive distortion leading to the negative belief or self-talk.

    Example: "I'm always nervous when I have to speak in front of people (Over-Generalization). I stumbled over my words so much last time that the audience will think I'm stupid (Mental Filter and Jumping to Conclusions)."

3. Replace the cognitive distortion with a rational, more realistic thought.

    Example: "I get a little nervous before public speaking, but that is just my body's natural adrenaline reaction preparing for a stressor. Although I stumbled through some words last time, I know my presentation wasn't all that bad and nobody probably even noticed the stumble."

4. Replace the negative belief or self-talk with a positive belief.

    Example: "As long as I keep practicing, I will continue to improve my presentation skillset and people will begin to see me as a good public speaker."

Use the following chart to practice changing your own negative beliefs, self-talk, or emotions in to positive ones.

| Negative Belief/ Self-Talk/Emotion | |
|---|---|
| Cognitive Distortion | |
| Replacement Thought | |
| Replacement Belief/ Self-Talk | |

# How Your Emotions Affect Your Learning

Have you ever been in a situation where your emotions undermined your motivation to learn? Maybe you struggled with a concept on a test, or made a lower grade than you wanted. The next time you tried to study, did the frustration of those struggles lead to feelings of disinterest or defeat? Or maybe you have felt that the format of a class isn't really your favorite, or that the faculty person came across as uncaring. Did you feel less interested in learning the material, or did you feel you no longer cared about that class because of that experience?

Those are examples of ways in which negative emotions can negatively impact your motivation to learn. We imagine you can think of other examples as well.

---

## DISCOVERY

1. Think of a time when you felt strong negative emotions about a class or an assignment. What was the experience that led to those emotions?

   _____

   _____

   _____

2. How did your negative emotions affect your motivation and/or performance in that class? What was the end result?

   _____

   _____

   _____

---

When you have a positive frame of mind and positive emotions about learning, on the other hand, these can increase your motivation to learn. In fact, they become a positive cycle in which your positive emotions lead to increased motivation, which leads to increased learning, which leads to better performance, which leads back to more positive emotions.

## Figure 6.2:    Emotions and Learning.

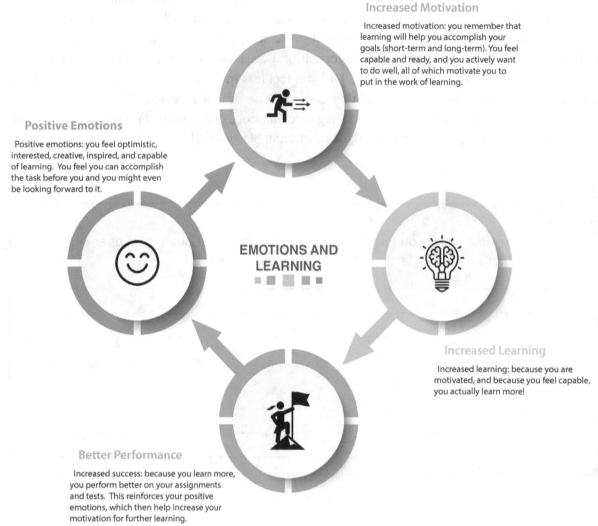

**Increased Motivation**

Increased motivation: you remember that learning will help you accomplish your goals (short-term and long-term). You feel capable and ready, and you actively want to do well, all of which motivate you to put in the work of learning.

**Positive Emotions**

Positive emotions: you feel optimistic, interested, creative, inspired, and capable of learning. You feel you can accomplish the task before you and you might even be looking forward to it.

**EMOTIONS AND LEARNING**

**Increased Learning**

Increased learning: because you are motivated, and because you feel capable, you actually learn more!

**Better Performance**

Increased success: because you learn more, you perform better on your assignments and tests. This reinforces your positive emotions, which then help increase your motivation for further learning.

---

**DISCOVERY**

1. Think of a time when you felt positive emotions about a class or an assignment. What was the experience that led to those emotions? How did your positive emotions affect your motivation and/or performance in that class? What was the end result?

   _____

   _____

   _____

Why is it sometimes difficult to stay motivated? Students report that in order to remain motivated they need to see value in what they are doing, they need an environment that feels supportive, and they need to believe in their ability to succeed. If you are struggling with motivation, take the time to analyze this problem along these lines:

- **Value**: How important is this activity to me? Which short-term goals will it help me accomplish? Which long-term goals will it help me accomplish?
- **Environment**: how supported do I feel in the learning environment? If you feel you need more support than you are getting, take the initiative to reach out in these ways:
  — Talk with the instructor about any questions you have about course material. Reach out to your instructor by attending their office hours, or sending them email. If they are free to chat after class, this may be a good time to speak with them as well.
  — Seek out additional support from a Graduate Assistant assigned to your class
  — Seek out additional support at your college's center for student success or student support. Tutors, academic coaches, peer mentors and other supportive personnel may be available to you.
  — Reach out to your classmates to join a study group. Or, invite others to create a study group with you! If you are struggling, it is likely that others are as well.
- **Belief that you can succeed:** remember the importance of mindset, and the difference between experiencing failures as temporary setbacks (growth mindset) instead of permanent roadblocks. If you are overwhelmed with feelings of failure, this is a time to lean on supportive friends and family, and consider speaking with your college advisor or even with a counselor or therapist. Also, be sure you are taking good steps toward self-care on a daily basis.

## Your Network and Emotional Fuel

When you get overwhelmed and anxious, or when you doubt your ability to succeed, it can be like running out of gas on a road trip. Without gas, oil, and transmission fluid, your car will not run. If you try to force it to run without these fluids, you will damage the engine. In a similar way, you need emotional fuel to function well. This fuel provides the energy you need to move down the road toward your goals.

Your network is an essential source of this emotional fuel, and it is all around you! The relationships that you form with others provide emotional fuel in the form of comfort and support, guidance, wisdom, encouragement and inspiration. Different members of your network will help fuel you in different ways, which is why it is healthy and helpful to develop a robust and varied network.

People in your network could include:

- **Role Models** who are doing what you would like to do.
- **Mentors** who listen to you, coach you and invest their time and energy in you.
- **Inner Circle**, who are the closest to you, understand you deeply, who you trust implicitly
- **Mentees** who learn from you, people you are guiding and coaching.
- **Partners** who travel along with you and hold you accountable.
- **Heroes** who you look up to and admire.

## DISCOVERY

1.  Complete the following diagram by filling in the names of people who fit each category for you. Note that this diagram is based not on our more automatic categories (like "family members" or "friends") but instead on the quality and style of the relationship. For example, you might have a sister who is part of your inner circle or she might be more of a mentor. Someone you study with routinely might be more of a partner who holds you accountable, or more of a mentee who receives guidance from you. If you have several people in one category, and no-one in other categories, that's ok! The purpose of this exercise is to identify your network as it currently stands:

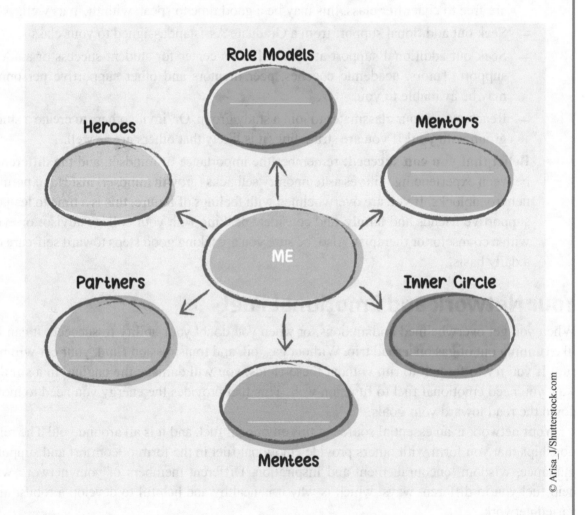

2.  What parts of my network are already robust, with several people listed? What parts are thinner, with few or no people? What could I do to grow the thinner parts of my network? How do the people currently in my network help provide me emotional fuel?

    _____

    _____

    _____

"For me personally, I joined a sorority coming into college. While I know Greek life is not for everyone, it is crucial to build a network right off the back whether that is through extracurriculars, roommates, or even just classes. My sorority, along with some clubs I joined, supplied me an abundance of friends, study partners, and mentors, although I definitely needed to also develop relationships with my professors and advisor. By attending office hours, you are able to engage with your teachers and build that aspect of your network. As for getting connected with your advisor, try to contact the same one for all your questions because they will start to recognize you and know your specific situation and help. My network has helped me in a number of ways from cheering me up when I miss home to providing me numerous leadership opportunities, but perhaps more amazing is how I have been able to support those around me. For example, just driving someone to the airport can mean a lot when we are all out here at college alone, so by being someone who can even marginally make other peoples' lives easier is extremely rewarding to me personally."

— Mae F., freshman, Management

"One of the most helpful and important people in my network were my professors. In order to build those relationships, I made sure I attended classes regularly and that the professor saw me there. I am not one to ask or answer questions in class so it can be difficult to be noticed by the professor especially in a big class. This was my biggest problem. I was very intimidated at the idea of talking to professors and actually having a relationship with them. I took the necessary steps to overcome this challenge. Every once in a while, I would go to the professor to talk about a topic from class that really interested me, and how I would like to move forward. My professors were later able to recommend internship and job opportunities that they saw would be a good fit for me."

— Oreoluwa A., senior, Chemical Engineering

# Overcoming Delays and Detours to Achieving Your Goals

We have all experienced construction zones while traveling. Though necessary, construction zones can delay our arrival at our destination by causing us to stop in traffic, take a detour, or use alternate routes. We can become frustrated with construction zones because of these deviations from our intended path, but we also understand that the construction zone doesn't last forever, and we will still get to our destination, eventually.

Just as you are not entirely in control while traveling, there are times where events outside of your control will also disrupt your college journey. No matter how organized you are, and how well you plan ahead during your college experience, you must recognize that not everything is under your control. You can expect delays and detours during your college journey. These disruptions may be as small as not passing your first math quiz, or as large as the COVID-19 global pandemic that forced students to learn virtually. The question is, how you will respond to delays and disruptions as they happen? If you develop your emotional intelligence and learn to identify and manage your emotions effectively, and if you learn to identify cognitive distortions that can negatively impact your thinking, you are much more likely to overcome disruptions, roadblocks and other "construction zones" as they take place.

## DISCOVERY

Below you will find a list of common disruptions you may experience during your college journey. Where the negative responses or positive solutions are left blank, insert them based on your experience and knowledge. At the bottom of the chart, add an additional 3 disruptions you think you personally might face and how you will successfully overcome them.

| Disruption | Negative Response | Positive Response |
| --- | --- | --- |
| You come down with strep throat and your doctor says you can't go to class for a week. | You view the diagnosis as a mid-semester vacation and allow yourself to get behind. | Contact your instructor to let them know, make sure you are getting class notes from a peer, and continue to work as possible. |
| Your psychology instructor doesn't respond quickly to emails and you have a question about the upcoming test. | You blame the instructor for not being responsive, don't get your question answered, and fail the test. | |
| Your instructor has to go on bed-rest and is unable to teach class in-person for the second half of the semester. | | |
| You have an unsupportive family member who thinks you are wasting your time going to college. | | |
| | | |
| | | |
| | | |

© F Armstrong Photography/Shutterstock.com

"I have always loved math and I have always been very good at math. Last semester I took an upper-level math class and I really struggled with it. It wasn't your average math class with numbers, it was proofs, proving how and why a math problem works the way it does. I didn't do well on the first test so before the second test I went to the professor's office hours to ask some questions to better prepare myself. While I was there, he basically told me if I didn't get it by now, I wasn't going to. I took this comment personally. I vowed to study more than I ever had before in order to do well in that class. I ended up with a solid A as my final grade."

— Kenzie B., senior, Mechanical Engineering

"I ended up needing to change my major to be more realistic and align with new goals that I set after my first semester. I had to change my goals for college as well as my initial career goal to be an entrepreneur. During a brief break from school, I used my time to focus on my strengths, think, develop my "plan B", and an action plan to attack it by changing my major and my career path. It was the best decision I could have made."

— Tyqueisha F., junior, Consumer Sciences

# Building Resilience

When you have to make a detour or are delayed from reaching your goals, you may experience a rush of uncertainty, negative thoughts, or strong emotions. As human beings we have a tendency to adapt to stressful situations over time, a process known as resiliency. Some people are naturally more resilient than others, but everyone can take steps to build resilience so that you can better cope in times of adversity or stress. Just like learning, building resilience doesn't just happen overnight! It takes time, practice, and intentionality. Even the most resilient people still experience distress some of the time. Their resilience means they have developed skillsets to overcome that distress. Below are some tips for developing resilience according to the American Psychological Association:

1. **Build Connections** with understanding and empathetic individuals or groups. Accepting help and making connections with others is better than isolation.

2. **Foster Wellness** by taking care of yourself physically and emotionally. As you will learn, stress is physical as well as emotional, and finding time to exercise and get healthy amounts of rest is beneficial. Avoiding negative outlets such as drugs, alcohol, or other substances is a good idea as well.

3. **Find Purpose** by focusing on your goals or through self-discovery, or by proactively identifying how you can avoid distress in the future. Examples may include focusing on academics, finding a new hobby or something else you enjoy, or helping others through service opportunities. These steps can help you focus on the positives in your life, while providing a broader perspective.

4. **Embrace Healthy Thoughts** by accepting change, maintaining a hopeful outlook, and learning from the past. Avoid catastrophic thinking and work to understand that you can overcome *any* stressful situation. Do your best to avoid putting yourself in situations that are likely to result in a similar, distressing outcome.

5. **Seek Help** from a professional if your distress is long-lasting. Your college or university has licensed professionals who can guide you in your path toward building resilience and getting back on track!

One benefit to adversity is that when we face it, we have the opportunity for significant personal growth. I would bet that everyone reading this textbook has at one time faced adversity, and has become a better person because of it.

**DISCOVERY**

1. Write about a time when you experienced a stressful situation and your resilience was tested.

_____

_____

_____

2. Was I proactive in overcoming the situation or did my distress linger?

_____

_____

_____

3. Would you do something different next time? If so, what?

_____

_____

_____

© Krakenimages.com/Shutterstock.com

## Saying "No"

Saying "no" can be difficult. Especially when it comes to friends and family, we often feel that if we do say "no" we might be letting someone down or we might miss out on something fun. There will be times during your college experience when you have a decision to make between doing something you would rather do (e.g., play video games, watch a movie, or attend a social gathering) and something that you should do (e.g., go to class or study). As long as you maintain balance and practice good self-management skills, you can always find time for both the fun stuff and the necessary stuff. In any case, you must be prepared to say "no" when you need to.

Other situations you may need to consider saying "no" to are taking on responsibilities that are not, and do not need to be yours. We all have responsibilities to our friends and families, but sometimes friends or family members do not understand the time commitments and responsibilities you have as a college student. When you enrolled in college you made an investment in your future, and you should do everything you can to reap the rewards of it. While at college, if you still find yourself having to solve problems back home, or spending a lot of time supporting friends and family that could otherwise be used to help you achieve YOUR goals, you may need to put your own needs first. This may include telling others, even those close to you, that putting their needs before your own must change.

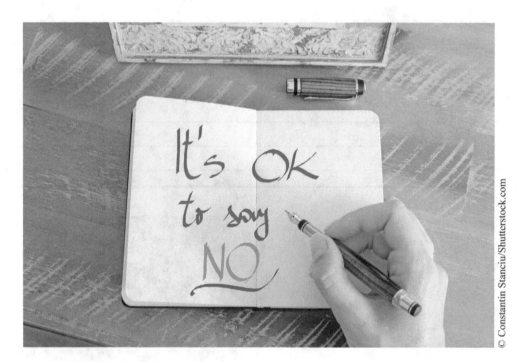

© Constantin Stanciu/Shutterstock.com

# Making Effective Decisions

While you cannot control all events, nor the behaviors of others, you can control your response to those individuals and events, and you should consider all options before responding. No matter the event, and no matter how serious it is, there is almost always a solution to keep you on a pathway to achieving your goals, even if that pathway causes delays or the use of an alternative route. One way to help yourself make the best decision when at a crossroads is to implement the following guiding process for making an effective decision:

Guidelines for Making Effective Decisions

1. Identify the details of your present situation as well as current and potential future barriers that may disrupt your plans.

2. Make a list of all of your possible choices or responses to the situation, as well as the likely outcomes of each.

3. Identify your choices or responses that are realistic and that you will commit to.

4. Make a plan, including a timeline with actions you will take and deadlines for taking them.

DISCOVERY

1. Identify a time when you did not use a procedure for making an informed decision and instead reacted with impulse. What was the outcome?

_____

_____

_____

2. Now identify a time when you did use a procedure for making an informed decision. What was the outcome?

_____

_____

_____

Now, let's practice with a decision you will soon need to make.

1. Identify the decision to be made
2. List ALL of your possible choices
3. Circle the choices that are realistic and you can commit to, but also best help you achieve your goals.
4. Finalize your decision by rewriting your best option, as well as when you will commit to actively responding

Current decision to be made: _____

_____

_____

| Response | Likely Outcome |
|---|---|
|  |  |
|  |  |
|  |  |
|  |  |
|  |  |

Choice you will commit to, including when you will actively respond:

_____

_____

# Overcoming Anxiety and Stress

We all experience stress and anxiety in our lives and we must all come to terms with that reality. No matter what you do, you will never completely rid yourself of stress or anxiety. Instead, you should learn to manage it. In Chapter 2, you learned how overcoming stress is beneficial for better learning. Persistent stress and anxiety can have other negative effects on you as well, including psychological consequences such as difficulty managing strong emotions in general, anger, depression, and memory loss. Physical consequences of persistent stress include headaches or body aches, high blood pressure, sexual dysfunction, irritable bowel, and others. In fact, according to the American Medical Association, stress is any interference that disturbs a person's mental or physical wellbeing. When we become stressed, our bodies release hormones that prepare us for a "fight, flight, or freeze" reaction that include immediate physical responses such as increased heart rate, differences in breathing, muscle tension, sleep deprivation, and others.

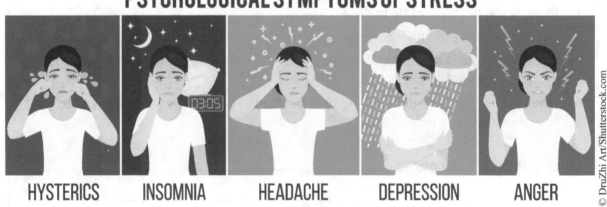

© DruZhi Art/Shutterstock.com

There are both healthy and unhealthy ways of reducing stress. Unfortunately, sometimes college students attempt to temporarily "escape" from their stressors by abusing substances such as alcohol or drugs, bingeing on television, overeating, or engaging in other compulsive behaviors to distract themselves. Several of these unhealthy "solutions" can actually lead to an increase in stress or anxiety over time.

Developing emotional intelligence and learning how to manage negative thinking habits can greatly reduce your stress and anxiety levels, as will understanding that not everything is in your control and developing the discipline to "let go" of things that are not, building resilience, learning to say "no," being hopeful, and intentionally making wise decisions. Understanding that you have the opportunity to CHOOSE different behaviors, thoughts, or responses to reduce stress or anxiety is a big, and important step.

The above solutions can be long-term and take practice. So, finding practical ways of reducing stress in the moment that work for you is a good idea. Below is a list of healthy stress-reducing strategies that can have an immediate impact.

- **Be prepared** – prepared for all classes, homework assignments, meetings, appointments, presentations, etc. Preparation builds confidence and reduces stress.

- **Be organized** – clutter has been proven to be a source for stress as it can make us feel overwhelmed. Keeping a clean and organized living and work space can be beneficial.

- **Utilize breathing techniques or meditation** – those experiencing stress or anxiety sometimes report shortness of breath, and are "chest-breathers" during stressful times. Deep, slow, breathing techniques can be useful for reducing stress immediately. Below is an example technique you can try.

- **Exercise** – cardio exercise such as jogging, biking, or playing basketball can greatly reduce stress but also allows you to feel joy.

- **Find joy** – whether it be playing with your pet, spending time with family or friends, reading a book for fun, listening to music, or attending a campus event, joy is an important factor for reducing stress.

- **Reduce the "noise" in your life** – with access to social media and news outlets 24 hours per day, 7 days per week, it is easy to become consumed with what is going on in the world, including perceived societal expectations that are impossible to live up to, or other negativity taking place in society. Much like physical "clutter" that can make us feel overwhelmed, so can social media "clutter" your mind and make you feel overwhelmed. Many feeling stress have reported that taking a break from social media and other outlets has been useful in reducing stress and anxiety.

## Breathing Technique for Reducing Anxiety

Often, people who are experiencing anxiety report shortness of breath. They often take small or shallow breathes (commonly referred to as chest-breathing) and do not fill their lungs completely. Taking deep breaths and filling your lungs has been proven to reduce anxiety significantly in that moment. Next time you feel anxious, try the breathing technique below:

1. Intertwine your fingers, and lift your arms straight up vertically above your head.
2. Take a deep breath in through your nose.
3. As slowly as you can, release the breath through your mouth.
4. Repeat as necessary.

# Hope

Hope is characterized as a feeling of expectation and desire for a certain thing to happen. When it comes to college success, research indicates that students with hope have higher GPAs, earn more credits, and are more likely to remain enrolled. According to the same research, students with hope indicate that there is an adult in their life who cares about their future, can think of many ways to get good grades, energetically pursue goals, are problem solvers, and are confident they will find a good job after graduation. This indicates positive thought processes lead to hope, and result in college success no matter students' intelligence, background, or major.

Hopeful students tend to believe they have the ability to make the future better than the present, tend to think positively, focus on their goals and success, are problem solvers, and overcome challenges by developing new pathways for success. Unfortunately, research indicates that only half of students in the United States are hopeful. The good news is that you can become hopeful by utilizing what you have learned about emotional intelligence, being intentional about avoiding cognitive distortions and replacing negative thoughts with positive ones, saying no, making wise decisions, and utilizing resources such as your academic advisor, faculty, or services such as those provided by your college or university's counseling center.

© vchal/Shutterstock.com

## Chapter Summary

Awareness and acceptance of your inner thoughts and emotions as they happen are the foundation becoming a mindful person. All students experience times of high emotion while in college, which may be a result of delays or detours to your goals that you must face, interactions with friends or family, or a result of "emotional baggage" that you allow to pile up within you. Successful students become mindful and develop their emotional intelligence, learn to say "no," are resilient and hopeful, and regularly complete personal wellness checks. Struggling students by contrast allow their emotions and thoughts to control them, are judgmental to themselves, and do not practice self-care. Mindfulness can be a great tool for improving your inner peace, your relationships with others, and your college and lifelong success, but it is up to you to find it.

## End-of-Chapter Activities

### I. Wellness Check

## WELLNESS CHECK

Use the following wellness check-in to determine how you are doing in terms of self-care. Circle the statement that best represents your current practices

| | |
|---|---|
| – I avoid sugary beverages such as sweetened coffee/tea, sodas, and juices | Always \| Sometimes \| Rarely \| Never |
| – I limit my consumption of alcohol and mind-altering substances | Always \| Sometimes \| Rarely \| Never |
| – I am mindful of caloric intake when eating out | Always \| Sometimes \| Rarely \| Never |
| – I eat at least 5 fruits and vegetables per day OR I fill half my plate with fruits and veggies at every meal | Always \| Sometimes \| Rarely \| Never |
| – I bike or walk to class or work | Always \| Sometimes \| Rarely \| Never |
| – I do something physically active during quick study breaks | Always \| Sometimes \| Rarely \| Never |
| – I workout or play a sport regularly | Always \| Sometimes \| Rarely \| Never |
| – I notice when my body is showing signs that I am stressed or anxious | Always \| Sometimes \| Rarely \| Never |
| – I take steps to alleviate stress when I am feeling stressed or anxious | Always \| Sometimes \| Rarely \| Never |
| – I do deep breathing or meditation on a daily basis | Always \| Sometimes \| Rarely \| Never |
| – I have friends and/or family I can talk to regularly, who help lower my feelings of stress or anxiety | Always \| Sometimes \| Rarely \| Never |
| – I try to do something that makes me happy every day | Always \| Sometimes \| Rarely \| Never |
| – I give myself an hour to relax and wind down before bed | Always \| Sometimes \| Rarely \| Never |
| – I keep my bed as a sleep-only (not study and work) zone | Always \| Sometimes \| Rarely \| Never |
| – I sleep 7 to 8 hours each night | Always \| Sometimes \| Rarely \| Never |
| – I keep my room cool during sleep hours | Always \| Sometimes \| Rarely \| Never |

Which elements of your self-care are going really well? Which were points of focus over the past month, which have improved since your last check-in? Which ones are not going so well? Build on your progress by choose one or two new points that you wish to improve on and commit to those for the next 3 weeks. You could even create a SMART goal for them! At the end of 3 weeks, you will likely find that they have become easy and habitual for you.

If you did not fully accomplish your goals from the last check-in, you could also recommit to those goals. In that case, take the time to analyze why you did not succeed at those goals last time – were they too broad or nonspecific? Were they not realistic or achievable? Once you have identified the issues, reframe or reconstruct your goals to make them SMARTer (specific, measurable, achievable, relevant, and time-bound). Then, try again for a month, starting now!

Above all, be kind and understanding to yourself. Wellness goals are intended to help you take good care of yourself, not to give you a reason to feel badly about how you are doing. Remember that personal wellness is a journey, and we all run into bumps in the road. When you hit a bump, determine what happened without judging yourself harshly, and then consider what will most help you move toward better self-care.

# References

Downing, S. (2017). *On course: Strategies for creating success in college and in life* (Study Skills Plus ed.). Cengage. ISBN-13: 978-1305397484

Elmore, T. (2018). *Habitudes: For self-leadership.* Growing Leaders Inc. ISBN 978-0-9792940-5-1

Elmore, T. (2014). *Habitudes: For the journey.* Poet Gardner Publishers. ISBN 978-0-9886201-0-0

Lopez, S. J. (2009). Hope, academic success, and the Gallup student poll. *Gallup student poll: America's promise alliance.* Gallup, Inc.

McGuire, S., & McGuire, S. (2018). *Teach yourself how to learn: Strategies you can use to ace any course at any level.* Stylus Publishing. ISBN 9781620367551

(2012). American Psychological Association. *Building your resilience.* https://www.apa.org/topics/resilience

(2021). Mindfulness. *Psychology Today.* Sussex Publishers, LLC. https://www.psychologytoday.com/us/basics/mindfulness

(2021). American Psychological Association. *Stress relief is within reach.* https://www.apa.org/topics/stress

## Chapter 7

# Continuing the Journey

| Choices of Successful Students | Choices of Struggling Students |
|---|---|
| 1. Revisit their goals frequently to keep themselves on track. | 1. Lose track of their goals or forget about them completely. |
| 2. Actively seek ways to stay motivated throughout the course of the academic term. | 2. Give in to low motivation or give up on engaging with their studies before the academic term ends. |
| 3. Take responsibility for their own progress toward their goals, even when challenges arise. | 3. Fail to take responsibility for their own responses to challenges. |
| 4. Meet with their academic advisor for course planning, which may include taking advantage of summer or winter term opportunities. | 4. Ignore academic advising invitations and are late to register, limiting their choices for classes in the upcoming term. |
| 5. By the end of their first semester, begin the process for researching housing options for their second year. | 5. Wait until the last moment to secure housing for their second term, resulting in limited choices and potential poor (or costly) experience. |
| 6. Are proactive in securing financial aid by completing financial aid applications when they become available. | 6. Ignore financial aid opportunities and end up paying more out of pocket or having to take out more loans. |

## Introduction

As you get close to the end of your first term in college, or your first term at a college new to you, you have two major tasks before you: On the one hand, you need to focus on finishing strong in your classes for the current academic term. On the other, you need to go ahead and begin planning for the next term or even the next year. From an academic standpoint, you might need to meet with your academic advisor for the next term's course recommendations, you will definitely need to prepare for final exams, and you'll want to reflect on your first semester in an effort to continue to maintain or improve future academic performance. From a nonacademic standpoint, you may need to consider housing, and how you will pay for the next year. Think of the last few weeks of each term as a time not only to work toward a successful finish in your current classes and college experience, but to plan ahead for your next steps – academically, personally, residentially, and financially. Get in the habit of taking the steps outlined in this chapter at the end of every term until you graduate.

1. How would you assess your study habits?
2. How can you stay motivated in college for the long term?
3. What are some important considerations as your first term in college comes to an end?

# Revisiting Goals ⊛

In Chapter 2, you learned to set SMART goals. In Chapter 5, you learned how to refine those into content and process goals, and how to assess them periodically to make sure they were getting you where you wanted to be. When you create and assess your own goals, it can be like blazing a trail. You know you want to get from point A to point B, from the start of the semester to passing your classes at the end, and you are creating the trail that will get you there.

© finwal89/Shutterstock.com

Sometimes the steps you take move you in the right direction. Sometimes you realize you have gone off course, and you either retrace your steps and try again, or you use that as a new starting point to head in the right direction. In either case, you learn from the experience as you consider where you are, determine or assess how you got there, and then refocus on where you want to be. The assessment step is essential because it requires you to think through your own process, allowing you to keep going with what was working for you, drop the pieces that were not working, and add some new things to try as you hone your skill.

© Dave Allen Photography/Shutterstock.com

As you near the end of the academic term, it is time to assess your progress toward your academic goals. You will have an opportunity to do so in depth at the end of this chapter. Closely related to this, it is time for one more serious assessment of your learning skills and habits, before you submit final projects and take final exams.

## Study Habits Self-Assessment

Think about your study habits across the board, for each of your classes. Circle the best response to each of the following questions, considering all of your classes:

- I attend every class meeting.                    Always | Often | Sometimes | Rarely | Never

- I complete assigned readings before each class meeting.                    Always | Often | Sometimes | Rarely | Never

- I take notes during every class meeting.                    Always | Often | Sometimes | Rarely | Never

- I review my notes within 24 hours after each class meeting.                    Always | Often | Sometimes | Rarely | Never

- I have homework, assignments, tests and exams marked in my calendar.                    Always | Often | Sometimes | Rarely | Never

- I have study time for specific classes and topics marked in my calendar.                    Always | Often | Sometimes | Rarely | Never

— I consult my calendar daily throughout the week.

Always | Often | Sometimes | Rarely | Never

— I begin study for tests at least 3 to 5 days in advance.

Always | Often | Sometimes | Rarely | Never

— My test/exam preparation includes reviewing my notes from tests and readings.

Always | Often | Sometimes | Rarely | Never

— My test/exam preparation includes reviewing assigned readings.

Always | Often | Sometimes | Rarely | Never

— My test/exam preparation includes practice working problems.

Always | Often | Sometimes | Rarely | Never

— My test/exam preparation includes reviewing previous tests to discover which areas need additional study.

Always | Often | Sometimes | Rarely | Never

— I take good care of myself on a daily basis (nutrition, exercise, sleep, relaxation).

Always | Often | Sometimes | Rarely | Never

— I make time for social activities and connect with my friends and family every week.

Always | Often | Sometimes | Rarely | Never

— I do something for my own well-being, to "recharge my batteries" every week.

Always | Often | Sometimes | Rarely | Never

## DISCOVERY

1. What patterns do you see in the self-assessment above? What would you say has gone especially well in terms of your study and self-care habits this semester or term? What would you say needs improvement?

_____

_____

_____

*Dive deeper with the Goals Self-Assessment and Finals Study Planner in the End-of-Chapter activities.*

© Sumandaq/Shutterstock.com

## Staying Motivated ⊕

All the way back in Chapter 1 you learned about grit, that combination of passion and hard work that predicts success much more than innate talent or inborn ability. You may have experienced your level of grit, or determination, shift somewhat over the course of the term. You may have been tired at times, and that may have zapped your motivation. Or you may have had experiences that shook your determination and drive, or caused you to question your resolve.

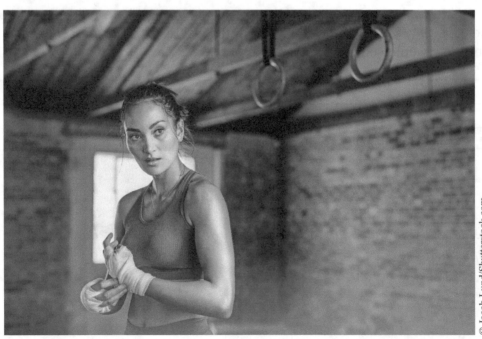

© Jacob Lund/Shutterstock.com

Now is the time to set aside your doubts and frustrations, dig back in, and refuel your motivation. At 2 to 3 weeks before the end of term, you see the light at the end of the tunnel, and you know you are going to get there. The question is *how* you will get there, and you are the one who gets to decide that.

Dr. Angela Duckworth states in *Grit: The Power of Passion and Perseverance* that grit depends on a particular kind of hope. You may hope for sunnier weather tomorrow, or you may hope that your path ahead will become clearer. Those hopes are valuable if they help you have a positive outlook on life and help you embrace more of an optimistic attitude. Still, those hopes do not require any personal investment or responsibility. The sun always rises, whether we hope for it or not.

As mentioned in Chapter 6, hopeful students are those who replace negative thoughts and emotions with positive ones, and tend to do better in college. Of course, thinking positively alone will not result in higher GPAs and more credits earned – those require that you take action, and this action is the kind of hope that Dr. Duckworth describes. She states that it "rests on the expectation that our own efforts can improve our future" (169). The kind of hope she portrays does not depend on luck or changes in the weather, but on your own personal decision to make tomorrow better. This hope rests on your growth mindset, your belief that you can continue learning and growing, that you can continue improving your abilities. It also rests on your willingness to dedicate yourself, to work hard, and to be invested in the outcomes.

## DISCOVERY

1. What are my hopes for the end of this semester? What do I hope to achieve, academically and personally? What are the best possible outcomes I can envision?

   _____

   _____

   _____

2. Now that I have listed my hopes, what will I do to achieve those? What concrete steps have I already taken? What other steps do I need to take, to set those in motion? How will I go about taking those steps?

   _____

   _____

   _____

You may find that your hopes strongly reflect the SMART goals you set earlier in the term, or you may find that they go a little deeper or bring in new elements you were not thinking about earlier in the term. As a student new to the college experience in general, or new to a particular college or university, you have been through a great deal of growth and change since the beginning of the term. If your hopes and your goals have shifted, consider whether they now reflect your direction and wishes more accurately, in response to all you have been learning about yourself, about your college, and about the academic experience. Give yourself a pat on the back for all you have accomplished already, and all you have learned!

## When Your Motivation Needs a Boost

Do you feel your motivation wavering? Take these steps to recenter and refuel:

1. **Reconnect with your purpose**. Travel back in your mind to the first 2 to 3 weeks of this academic term, and recall the things that excited and motivated you about the experience. Remember what captured your enthusiasm and why you began this process. Revisit the SMART goals you set in Chapter 2 and the hopes you listed above. Take a moment to write down your purpose in terms of your initial enthusiasm and motivation, your goals, and your hopes. Think of this written item as your *statement of purpose*. After reading your statement of purpose back to yourself, take 5 deep breaths as you hold it in your mind. This is a way to practice mindfulness related to your sense of purpose. Take time to reconnect with your purpose in this way every day.

2. **Start with an easy step.** Are you overwhelmed by the number of things you need to complete? Are you tempted to procrastinate? Begin by "chunking" what you have to accomplish by breaking your goals down into manageable steps. For instance, "study for Chemistry 101 exam" may feel overwhelming, but breaking your review of materials into specific steps (such as "gather all materials", or "review notes on chapters 3 to 6" or "review vocabulary flashcards") and placing those in your calendar for specific study sessions will help the process feel more manageable. Then, begin with an easy step, like assembling your study materials into one place, tidying up your study zone, or organizing the first exam-preparation meeting with your study group. The first step may be the most difficult, but when you complete it, you will feel more able to keep going.

3. **Be accountable for your goals and your progress.** Accountability is an excellent motivator! Some students ask a friend or their study group to be accountability partners by stating their goals and then reporting honestly each day or each week (depending on the goals) about whether they accomplished what they had planned. Other students share similar information on social media and ask their network to help hold them accountable. Either way, the public commitment will help you feel more responsible for the goals you have set for yourself.

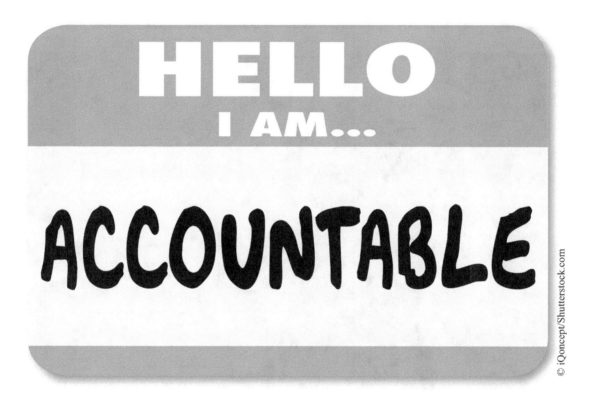

© iQoncept/Shutterstock.com

4. **Visualize yourself accomplishing your goals**. Close your eyes, take a deep breath in and out, and imagine yourself achieving the goals you have set for yourself. Hold the image in your mind through several breaths. While you keep the image in your mind, pay attention to your sensations. In your imagination, how do you feel about your accomplishment? Where are you? Who are you with? How are you going to celebrate? Like reconnecting with your purpose, visualizing yourself completing your goals is a mindful practice you can use every day.

5. **Reward yourself!** Think of something you will do to celebrate the end of the term. A reward could be a movie night or dinner out with friends, a long hike or walk in a beautiful area, a plan to explore an event venue, gallery, or live music you have been curious to hear, or a special treat you would enjoy. Some people like to set small rewards for each goal they accomplish, while others plan on a big reward for the larger goal of completing the academic term. Some people do both! Decide on the rewards that will both motivate you and help you tap into a feeling of celebration and achievement.

**DISCOVERY**

1. How would I like to reward myself for a job well done? List 2 to 3 specific rewards you would like to give yourself on completion of your goals this term.

_____

_____

_____

© fizkes/Shutterstock.com

"A big piece of advice I can offer is to plan well ahead for the final weeks of the term. Cramming for finals last minute never ends well, and your grades and sleep schedule will suffer if you do not plan accordingly. I learned early on during college that college is very different than high school in the way you need to approach your classes and study habits. I have found that spacing studying out over a period of several days to weeks before a test, especially a final exam, is the most beneficial. You retain the information better and perform better on exams. Another piece of advice is taking care of yourself both physically and mentally. You need to make sure you are getting enough sleep and eating balanced meals to ensure you are staying healthy and can perform optimally on exams. It can be hard to balance sleep and eating well during hectic finals week, but it is something I found can make a big difference. Sleep and eating healthy help with memory retention. I reward myself at the end of finals by doing something fun with friends and getting food from one of my favorite restaurants."

— Payton M., senior, Psychology

© Zviahintsev Denis/Shutterstock.com

## Passengers and Drivers

In Chapter 6, we compared the academic term to a road trip. You completed reflections on dealing with emotional baggage, keeping your emotional fuel tank full, how you deal with detours, and the like. We will return to the road trip metaphor here with this question: regarding your life, are you a *passenger* or a *driver*?

Tim Elmore uses the concept of "passengers and drivers" as a metaphor for self-leadership in *Habitudes: Images that Form Leadership Habits and* Attitudes. He states that when people are faced with life challenges, those who blame others for their problems are passengers in their own lives, while people who take responsibility for their attitudes toward challenges are drivers. If you are recently out of high school, it is possible that you have been a passenger for much of your life. It is fairly typical for children and teens to be "passengers" as their parents or guardians provide for them and make decisions over which they have little control. If you are a self-supporting adult, you are already experiencing what it is like to be a driver, as you provide for yourself and possibly others, and make decisions about every aspect of your life. Many college students are somewhere in between – not fully independent yet, but making many of their own decisions.

Whether you have been more of a passenger or a driver in terms of life decisions, everyone has the opportunity to be a driver, academically. In other words, everyone has the opportunity in college to set priorities and take responsibility for their goals, study habits, time management, work ethic, and attitude.

## DISCOVERY

1.  Considering your own goals, study habits, time management, work ethic, attitude, and other elements of your life as a college student, identify 2 to 3 areas in which you failed to be a "driver," allowing outside circumstances to determine your direction. Write those areas below.

    _____

    _____

    _____

2.  Now, for each area you identified above, list one decision you could make that would help you get back into the driver's seat and take responsibility for your direction.

    _____

    _____

    _____

"It is the most important thing to get back in the driver's seat. After an accident my first year, I had to withdraw from my classes. I felt so defeated but I didn't let my emotions win. I saved up and came back to finish the job. Your plans and goals don't give up on you, you give up on them! As Les Brown stated: 'If you fall try and land on your back because if you can look up you can get up.' I live by just that. As a first-generation student, I will not give up on my degree."

— Tyqueisha F., junior, Consumer Sciences

© Martin Novak/Shutterstock.com

"For me, the biggest adjustment in starting college was having to study for exams well in advance. Back in high school, I could usually learn a concept within 2 to 3 class days and barely study and still ace the test. But that is not how college works. I learned that the hard way. I had to adjust by beginning to review or study material for an exam at least a week or even two before the day of the exam. And since I started doing that, my exam grades improved drastically."

— Cody H., senior, Aerospace Engineering

## Preparing for Finals

A major activity for the last 2 to 3 weeks of every college term will be preparing for finals. In some ways, you have been preparing for them throughout the term as you incorporated the following activities and habits into your life:

- developing your own study habits and routines
- reading assigned materials
- attending class regularly
- taking notes based on lectures, videos, readings, etc.
- preparing for smaller tests and exams
- planning study time in your daily and weekly calendar
- taking good care of yourself

*All* of these activities represent an investment on your part. They have been helping you learn the material for your classes and have contributed to your current preparedness for final papers, projects, exams and the like.

If you have been doing the activities listed above 80% to 90% of the time, it is likely that you can enter this finals preparation phase with a degree of confidence and clarity about what you need to accomplish for a successful end of term.

If you started doing most of those activities but have slowed down or slacked off as the academic term wore on, now is the time to grind! With hard work and dedicated study, you may be able to make up for lost time. This is your time to focus, get organized, and keep your eyes on your goals to finish the academic term strong.

If you are currently saying "oh no!" (or something similar) and have been doing few or none of those activities, you may be facing a salvage operation. If you are in this situation, it's time for you to do a realistic assessment of what is needed and what is possible, and then devote yourself fully – heart, body and mind – to doing the very best you can.

The Finals Study Planner at the end of this chapter will take you step-by-step through planning effectively for final exams. For best results, have your finals plan completed a full 2 weeks or more before the beginning of finals week.

"My advice for the last couple weeks of the semester around finals time is to get enough sleep. You can pull an all-nighter, but in the end, those hurt you more than they help. Study ahead of time so that the night before a final you can get enough sleep so your brain can perform better during the exam. Another piece of advice, especially for finals, is to get together a study group. If there's a concept you don't understand, chances are if you get with a group of 4 or 5 people, one of them will understand it and can help you come to understand it. This can also help with doing practice problems and making sure everyone is getting the same answers."

— Cody H., senior, Aerospace Engineering

## Registration and Advising at the End of Term

Depending on when you are reading this chapter, you may have already been invited for academic advising for next term. If not, you should find out what your college's or university's expectations are for academic advising, and how you can meet with an advisor for upcoming term course recommendations. Assuming you successfully complete all of your current classes, you can probably just follow the curriculum map for your major and identify the next progression of classes you need to take, then meet with your advisor to confirm those choices. If, however, you had to drop a class or will not pass one or more of your current classes, you may need to consider retaking those courses and adjusting your academic plan. If this is the case, you should make an appointment with your academic advisor.

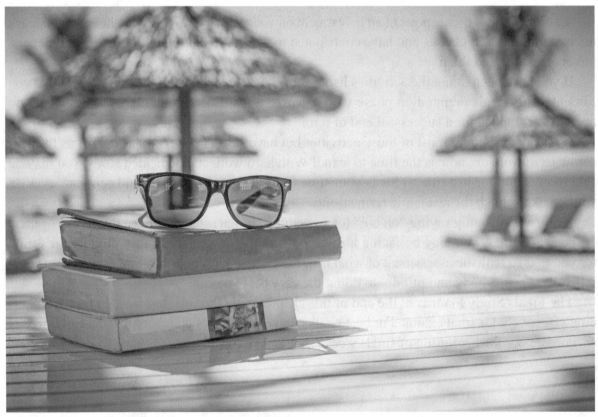

## Summer and Winter Terms

Many colleges and universities include the summer or winter as part of their "regular" enrollment and enrolling over the summer or winter months are normal practice. The more traditional college or university student, however, focuses on fall and spring terms for when they plan on taking the majority of their classes. Savvy college students at these institutions at least consider summer or winter term classes as well. Generally, colleges and universities offer multiple summer or winter terms. Summer terms may include a short, 3- to 4-week terms just after the spring term ends often known as an "interim" term, as well as 4- to 5-week terms in June and July, and 8- to 10-week terms that last most of the summer. Winter terms are generally fewer, shorter, and have less course options available than summer, but can still be beneficial for students.

Summer and winter terms are a great way for you to get ahead, or catch up on your 4-year plan if you had to drop a class(es) during the fall or spring terms. It is not uncommon for students to utilize summer and winter terms and graduate in fewer than 4 years. Summer classes generally have the benefits of smaller class sizes, more individualized opportunity with faculty, and less out-of-the-classroom distractions than do "regular" term classes. However, summer and winter terms are generally shorter than regular fall or spring terms and will still include the same amount of material as a longer term. This results in longer class meetings and class meetings on more days of the week. Students taking summer or winter term classes must absorb the same amount of material in a shorter amount of time. Additionally, some resources may not be as readily available in the summer or winter as would be during fall or spring terms. If you are considering taking classes during a summer or winter term, you should consult with your academic advisor.

# Making Housing Plans for Next Year ⊛

If you are attending a college or university that requires you to stay in a residence hall your first term or your first year, this may be a time when you need to be thinking about housing for your next year. A lot of variables need to be considered, including whether you want a roommate (and who that might be), if you want to live on or off campus, and how you will pay for housing. Whether your housing options are plentiful or competitive, beginning your search early will give you the best chance of securing the best housing option for you.

There are many benefits to on-campus housing, so much so that some colleges and universities require it for students beyond their first year. Benefits to living on campus are vast, and include easier access to campus resources, events, and other opportunities, making friends and building community, not having to worry about bills for electricity, water, trash pickup, and Wi-Fi, facility upkeep, or sense of security. Research also indicates that students who live on campus complete more credits and have higher GPAs, show greater gains in student development and self-esteem, are more likely to graduate from their original institution, and graduate with greater frequency. Also, as you continue at your college or university, you may have access to residence halls with better amenities and location than you did as a first-time student.

If you are living in a university-run residence hall, you will likely be notified by housing staff when upcoming year housing applications open either through campus email or other advertisements around the community. If you are interested in on-campus housing and don't know by the end of your first term when upcoming year applications are available, check with housing staff or online to find out.

Off-campus housing options have benefits too, such as different freedoms, privacy, and housing options. Depending on your needs, off-campus housing may be a better option for you. As was mentioned in Chapter 3, if housing cost is a concern for you, you should be a smart consumer by doing your research about living either on or off campus. On campus housing packages are generally a lump sum that include utilities, Wi-Fi, parking, dining packages, and other amenities that off-campus housing does not. Be careful not to become convinced that off-campus is cheaper simply based on a low monthly rent rate. An off-campus lease could may be 12 months and include months that you don't plan on living in town. It is difficult to provide an example cost-comparison because many variables will dictate costs and will depend on the college or university and community, but doing research can help you make an informed decision.

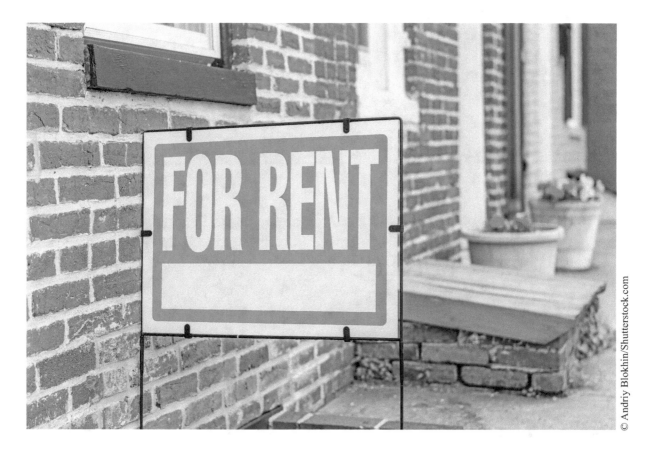

© Andriy Blokhin/Shutterstock.com

## Accessing Financial Aid for the Next Academic Year

As indicated in Chapter 3, for each academic year you plan to receive federal financial aid (federal loans, grants, Federal Work Study) you will need to fill out the Free Application for Federal Student Aid (FAFSA). You should plan to renew your FAFSA as early as you can, which is generally in October of the year prior to the academic year for which you are seeking aid (e.g., apply in October 2024 for funding to cover the academic year 2025–2026).

Also indicated in Chapter 3, you should consider applying for grants or scholarships provided by your college or university. Application availability for college or university grants or scholarships differ, but are also generally available the year prior, sometimes as early as by the time the semester opens. For example, you may be able to apply in August 2024 for funding to cover the academic year 2025–2026). These applications generally close in the spring of the year prior (e.g., application for funding 2025–2026 may expire in March 2025) so getting your scholarship application in now might be a good idea.

## Final Thoughts

Congratulations on reaching the end of your academic term! We hope it was a good experience for you. Even more, we hope you learned something along the way about your resilience, your abilities, your strengths, and areas you are still working on. We hope you connected with others and found community, and that you have a better idea of where to go for help and resources when you need them. We hope you found out that you are capable college students, and we hope you will find ways to transform experiences of failure (we all have them) into opportunities to learn what did and did not work for you, and try again.

Please continue to rely on this workbook in future terms until you have mastered and internalized your own strategies for college success. Along the way, share those strategies with others! It has been a privilege to walk through the academic term with you, and we wish you all the best.

– Dr. Brian J. Gorman

– Dr. Jennifer L. Roth-Burnette

# End-of-Chapter Activities

## I. Goals Self-Assessment.

Return to the SMART goals you created in Chapter 2. Use the following chart to assess your own progress on your SMART goals. Remember that SMART goals are specific, measurable, achievable, relevant, and time-bound.

| SMART Goal List | How close am I to completing this goal? (for example, 83% or "about halfway" or "done!") | Does this goal need to be adjusted or refined? If so, how? Describe changes below. | Do I need longer to complete this goal? If so, how long? | How I rewarded or will reward myself for completing this goal. |
|---|---|---|---|---|
|  |  |  |  |  |
|  |  |  |  |  |
|  |  |  |  |  |
|  |  |  |  |  |

## II. Staying Motivated.

You can increase your clarity and self-accountability to keep your motivation high by writing down the ideas and concepts that motivate you. Choose two or more of the following brief writing exercises to lock in your motivation.

1.  Write your statement of purpose (from #1 under When Your Motivation Needs a Boost)

    _____

    _____

    _____

2.  Write a detailed description of your visualization (from #4 under When Your Motivation Needs a Boost). What have you just accomplished? What do you see? Where are you? How do you feel? Who are you with? How are you going to celebrate? What other details stand out to you?

    _____

    _____

    _____

3.  Write a quote or a phrase that inspires you and helps you feel motivated. This could be a phrase from a favorite role model, a quote from a book that inspired you, or something a trusted friend or relative said to uplift you.

    _____

    _____

    _____

4.  Create a personal mantra. Read over your goals, your statement of purpose, your vision for a successful future and give yourself at least 30 minutes to reflect deeply and focus both on the actions and the feelings you associate with these. Then find a brief "I" statement that captures the most important or most essential theme. For example, "I am strong and capable of the work ahead of me" or "I am responsible enough to achieve my goals" or "I will fearlessly push myself out of my comfort zone to ask for the help I need." Write your mantra below.

    _____

    _____

    _____

5.  Repeat your mantra to yourself morning, noon and night, and additionally when you begin to doubt yourself. You may find yourself making decisions that help you live into the way you have described yourself in your mantra.

_Take your motivational writing to the next level by putting any of the material you wrote above on a post-it or a notecard and placing it where you will see it daily, like your mirror or the refrigerator._

## III. Finals Study Planner.

## Finals Study Plan

**Fill out the following charts completely to draft your personalized study plan for finals.** The information you need includes information about each final (exam, project, paper or other assignment), your current grade, available resources, list of topics/concepts for each exam, study strategies you will use, and the last 2 to 3 weeks of tasks and assignments to finish each class.

| | Name of Class: | Name of Class: | Name of Class: | Name of Class: | Name of Class: |
|---|---|---|---|---|---|
| **Final Date/Due Date:** | | | | | |
| **Location of Final:** | | | | | |
| **Info. about final** *(is it an exam, online, project, paper, etc.?)* | | | | | |
| **Current grade in class:** (A, C+, 83, etc.) | | | | | |
| **Final grade info:** – % of grade? – cumulative or regular exam? | | | | | |
| **What grade do I want to make in this class?** | | | | | |
| **Is my ideal grade possible?** | | | | | |
| **What resources are available to me?** *(tutoring, review sessions, office hours, other)* | | | | | |
| **What days/times and locations can I access these resources?** | | | | | |

# Finals Study Plan

| List the main topics or concepts to review for each final, then rate your current knowledge level for each:<br>3 = know it<br>2 = sort of know it<br>1 = don't know it | Name of Class: | Name of Class: | Name of Class: | Name of Class: | Name of Class: |
|---|---|---|---|---|---|
| | Topic: _____ 3_ 2_ 1_ | Topic: _____ 3_ 2_ 1_ | Topic: _____ 3_ 2_ 1_ | Topic: _____ 3_ 2_ 1_ | Topic: _____ 3_ 2_ 1_ |
| | Topic: _____ 3_ 2_ 1_ | Topic: _____ 3_ 2_ 1_ | Topic: _____ 3_ 2_ 1_ | Topic: _____ 3_ 2_ 1_ | Topic: _____ 3_ 2_ 1_ |
| | Topic: _____ 3_ 2_ 1_ | Topic: _____ 3_ 2_ 1_ | Topic: _____ 3_ 2_ 1_ | Topic: _____ 3_ 2_ 1_ | Topic: _____ 3_ 2_ 1_ |
| | Topic: _____ 3_ 2_ 1_ | Topic: _____ 3_ 2_ 1_ | Topic: _____ 3_ 2_ 1_ | Topic: _____ 3_ 2_ 1_ | Topic: _____ 3_ 2_ 1_ |
| | Topic: _____ 3_ 2_ 1_ | Topic: _____ 3_ 2_ 1_ | Topic: _____ 3_ 2_ 1_ | Topic: _____ 3_ 2_ 1_ | Topic: _____ 3_ 2_ 1_ |
| | Topic: _____ 3_ 2_ 1_ | Topic: _____ 3_ 2_ 1_ | Topic: _____ 3_ 2_ 1_ | Topic: _____ 3_ 2_ 1_ | Topic: _____ 3_ 2_ 1_ |
| | Topic: _____ 3_ 2_ 1_ | Topic: _____ 3_ 2_ 1_ | Topic: _____ 3_ 2_ 1_ | Topic: _____ 3_ 2_ 1_ | Topic: _____ 3_ 2_ 1_ |
| | Topic: _____ 3_ 2_ 1_ | Topic: _____ 3_ 2_ 1_ | Topic: _____ 3_ 2_ 1_ | Topic: _____ 3_ 2_ 1_ | Topic: _____ 3_ 2_ 1_ |
| | Topic: _____ 3_ 2_ 1_ | Topic: _____ 3_ 2_ 1_ | Topic: _____ 3_ 2_ 1_ | Topic: _____ 3_ 2_ 1_ | Topic: _____ 3_ 2_ 1_ |
| | Topic: _____ 3_ 2_ 1_ | Topic: _____ 3_ 2_ 1_ | Topic: _____ 3_ 2_ 1_ | Topic: _____ 3_ 2_ 1_ | Topic: _____ 3_ 2_ 1_ |

# Finals Study Plan

| Ask yourself: | Name of Class: | Name of Class: | Name of Class: | Name of Class: | Name of Class: |
|---|---|---|---|---|---|
| *How will I prepare for the exam?* | | | | | |
| *How will I know when I'm "ready" to take it?* | | | | | |
| *What study strategies have been most effective for me this term?* | | | | | |
| **List the specific study strategies you will use to prepare for each final exam.** | | | | | |

Use the following chart to create your study plan for the last 3 weeks of term, including finals week.

# Finals Study Plan

| Day | Date (fill in) | Tasks to complete | Notes |
|-----|----------------|-------------------|-------|
| M   |                |                   |       |
| Tu  |                |                   |       |
| W   |                |                   |       |
| Th  |                |                   |       |
| F   |                |                   |       |
| Sa  |                |                   |       |
| Su  |                |                   |       |
| M   |                |                   |       |
| Tu  |                |                   |       |
| W   |                |                   |       |
| Th  |                |                   |       |
| F   |                |                   |       |
| Sa  |                |                   |       |
| Su  |                |                   |       |

# Finals Study Plan

| Day | Date (fill in) | Tasks to complete | Notes |
|-----|----------------|-------------------|-------|
|     |                | ✱ FINALS WEEK ✱   |       |
| M   |                |                   |       |
| Tu  |                |                   |       |
| W   |                |                   |       |
| Th  |                |                   |       |
| F   |                |                   |       |
| Sa  |                |                   |       |

Now that you have completed your finals study plan, you may realize that the end of the semester is going to be very full! You may find that you need to devote a great deal of time to prepare for your final exams. This is a time to tap into your courage and your inner strength, get in touch with your grit, and remember that you can do anything for 2 to 3 weeks!

In addition to the intensive work you will do to prepare for finals, be sure to take good care of yourself. Use this checklist daily:

- Get adequate sleep
- Take brief breaks to rest your brain and activate your body
- Drink plenty of water
- Eat nutritious food
- Do exercise that refreshes and restores you
- Take time to meditate or reflect on your goals and dreams, or visualize your success
- When you get frustrated, take a deep breath, drink some water, listen to some music you love, and/or walk away for a few minutes to calm your mind
- Connect with friends or family who lift your spirits
- Remind yourself that *you can do this*
- Reward yourself for a job well done!

## IV. Cost of Living Activity.

Create a comparison of anticipated costs of living on-campus versus off-campus.

| Living On-Campus | Living Off-Campus |
|---|---|
| Cost of housing total _____ | Rent per month _____ × _____ months = _____ |
| Cost of dining _____ | Groceries _____ × _____ months = _____ |
| Other costs _____ | Electricity _____ × _____ months = _____ |
| _____ | Water _____ × _____ months = _____ |
| _____ | Trash _____ × _____ months = _____ |
| _____ | Cable/stream _____ × _____ months = _____ |
| _____ | Internet/Wi-Fi _____ × _____ months = _____ |
| _____ | Other _____ × _____ months = _____ |
| _____ | Other _____ × _____ months = _____ |
| _____ | Other _____ × _____ months = _____ |
| Total cost _____ | Total cost _____ |

## References

Duckworth, A. (2016). *Grit: The power of passion and perseverance.* Scribner.

Elmore, T. (2018). *Habitudes: Images that form leadership habits and attitudes.* Growing Leaders, Inc.